Man has been fishing for trout and sal
time of the Ancient Greeks. Devising ev
of doing so, his rods, reels, lines a
fascinating ways.

With a delightful blend of wit and erudition, Conrad Voss Bark tells
the story of flyfishing, from the Macedonian 'plumes' of old to the
hairwing streamers of today.

He spotlights the sport's formative protagonists - Juliana Berners,
Robert Venables, Isaak Walton, Charles Cotton, Alfred Ronalds,
George Kelson, J. C. Mottram, Dr Bell, and many others, using his
journalist's skills to appraise the prevailing dogmas, the break-
throughs in tackle and to re-live the great debates and controversies,
including the famous Skues-Halford dispute.

Throughout, flyfishing is seen against the broader canvas of the
changing times in Britain, Ireland and North America.

Today there are new forces which are shaping flyfishing history:
water pollution, drift netting, over-kill, timeshare, catch-and-release
and the explosion of new materials from which tackle and flies are
made.

Not since Waller Hills' classic *History of Fishing for Trout* of 1921,
has a broad survey of this fascinating sport has been tackled with
such individual style and verve.

Conrad Voss Bark has had a distinguished career as a journalist
and parliamentary correspondent for the BBC. Since his retirement
as a political commentator, he has been angling correspondent for
The Times for many years and has written a number of fishing
books, including A Fly on the Water and The Encyclopaedia of
Flyfishing. He is therefore well equipped to take on the task of
documenting flyfishing, and he brings to his subject a depth of
understanding and experience that few can rival.

He lives within casting distance of the Tamar in Devon,where his
wife, Anne, runs the famous fishing hotel, The Arundell Arms at
Lifton.

A History of FLYFISHING

Conrad Voss Bark

Merlin Unwin Books

First published by Merlin Unwin Books, 1992

Paperback edition first published in 1994

MERLIN UNWIN BOOKS
21 Corve Street, Ludlow
Shropshire SY8 1DA
England

British Library Cataloguing in Publication Data
A catalogue record for this book is
available from the British Library
ISBN 1-873674-16-3

Designed and typeset by Karen Unwin and Tina Mulliner
Printed in Great Britain by Cambridge University Press

TO ANNE

the best of fishing companions

Contents

Introduction   xiii

1   The Macedonian Method   1

2   Wyngis of the Pertryche   11

3   Cromwell's General   17

4   Cotton, Walton and Barker   27

5   The Ludlow Doctor   37

6   Points of Departure   47

7   The Arrival of Ronalds   57

8   Butterflies for Salmon   64

9   Springs and Origins   75

10 The Dry Fly   83

11 Halford   93

12 Branche Line   101

13 Reservoirs of Poison   109

14 The Nymph Men   113

15 Bell's Bugs   119

16 The Legitimate Method   123

17 The American Influence   127

18 Return of the Plume   131

19 A Change of Flies   137

20 The Time of our Lives   141

Appendix

The Roman Plume   147

The Treatyse   147

The Venables Text   151

Charles Cotton's Flies   152

Scotcher of Chepstow   153

Alfred Ronalds   155

George Pulman and the Dry Fly   159

The Upstream Wet Fly   161

Kelson's Salmon Flies   163

The Dry and the Floating Fly   166

G.E.M. Skues   170

H.S. Hall and the Dry Fly   172

Dr H. Bell   173

Bibliography   175

Illustrations

Black and White Illustrations

1. Inflated bladder, 7th century BC   2

2. Manuscript of Dame Juliana Berners' *Treatyse*   13

3. Title page of the *Treatyse*   15

4. Robert Venables in armour   18

5. Title page of *The Experienced Angler*   25

6. Charles Cotton (National Portrait Gallery)   29

7. Isaak Walton's creel in the library of the
   Flyfishers' Club, London (John Tarlton)   32

8. Title page of Franck's *Memoir*   40

9. Title page of Brookes' *Art of Angling*   43

10. George Kelson, the Victorian angler   68

11. The Jock Scott   70

12. Richard Routledge of Carlisle   76

13. Viscount Grey (BBC Hulton picture library)   79

14. David Foster, author, *The Scientific Angler*   85

15. H. S. Hall (Flyfishers' Club)   89

16. Frederic M. Halford (Flyfishers' Club)   95

17. G. E. M. Skues (Flyfishers' Club)   98

18. Theodore Gordon (*Forest & Stream*)   103

19. Frank Sawyer   115

20. George Younger   117

21. Assorted 'flies'   129

22. Early tube fly (Hardy catalogue, 1957)   132

Colour Plates

(in order of appearance within colour section)

1. Macedonian 'plumes' to Bowlker's green drake
2. The pioneer reservoir patterns
3. The development of hair-wing salmon flies
4. The feather-wing and dry salmon flies
5. Dry flies, nymphs, spiders and mayflies
6. Plate from George Scotcher's *Fly Fisher's Legacy*, 1800
7. Plate from Alfred Ronalds' *Fly Fisher's Entomology*, 1836
8. Plate from George Kelson's *The Salmon Fly*, 1895

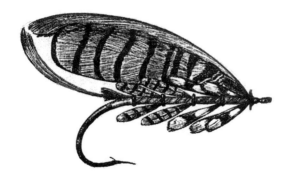

Introduction

Research into the history of flyfishing produces surprises. Many modern ideas have to be revised. One discovers that dry fly fishing did not start with Halford in the 1880s on the Test, that nymph fishing did not begin with the inventions of Skues and that Frank Sawyer was not the first to use weighted flies. Leaded pupae imitations were being tied by anglers 350 years ago, about the time that Charles I was beheaded in Whitehall.

In fact fly designs and the presentation of the fly have been little changed for hundreds of years. The Romans used streamer flies, called plumes, to fish Tyne and Thames during the Roman occupation of Britain. Beads were used to make bug-eyed flies for reservoir trout fishing in the 1960s, but the idea of doing so was first mooted some 200 years previously.

Upside-down flies, the ones with the hook point that floats uppermost which were recommended for taking difficult trout in the 1980s were first tied by a soldier of Cromwell's army in the 1660s. One could go on almost endlessly with examples of flies invented by one generation, then forgotten by the next and reinvented as something new, years and sometimes centuries later.

These variations on early themes determined to some extent, how much I am still not certain, the need to select from approximately 2,000 years of flyfishing history the significant stages of its development, the move from the Greeks to the Normans, to the first book in English on angling and the brilliant inventiveness of the 17th and 18th centuries which spurred and invigorated the thoughts and practices of the 19th.

There are certain times when the human spirit seems to burst with the enthusiasm and exhilaration of discovery and invention, when the whole atmosphere of the time is charged with the excitement of creation.

Such a time was in the 17th century when more books on angling were published than ever before, among them the wonderful picture of happy England in Isaak Walton's *Compleat Angler* which was written during the turmoil and horrors of civil war and religious persecution. At least three men - Venables, Cotton and Barker - represent the progress in flyfishing development of that time.

By the next century, the 18th, we are almost in sight of modern times with men like Stewart on the Borders fishing his spiders aloft upstream and the Bowlkers setting an example of skill and fly design on the Teme which lasted at least a hundred or more years. Of these two Stewart was a character of enormous charm and skill.

By the mid-1800s we are in reach of the first complete definition of how to fish the dry fly given by David Foster of Ashbourne in Derbyshire which for some curious reason was almost completely ignored by those who later became disciples of the great and autocratic Halford on the Test.

Halford laid down the principles of dry fly fishing which had been pioneered by Foster and others before him and was helped in the presentation of the fly by two great American inventions: the heavy, braided and oiled silk line and the split cane rod. These allowed for the first time a greater accuracy in the presentation of the fly to rising fish than had ever been possible with the light silk lines that had been in common use before.

It is right that at this stage, after a hundred years of apparent uncertainty, that the credit for inventing the true dry fly of the Test, the split-wing floater, should go to the Clifton school master, H. S. Hall, whose natural reticence contributed to a belief at the time that it was the invention of Marryat or Halford. The evidence for Hall which is given in full in the Appendix on page 172 is, I believe, conclusive.

The split-wing floater, however, had its day and is now largely overtaken in use and popularity by other fly designs which are based not on Halford's principle of exact imitation but on creating the illusion of an insect rather than a copy of it. Fly design has a fashionable as well as an ephemeral life which, to most flyfishers, is part of its fascination and attraction.

All the same it was rather sad that most of Halford's disciples, with a few honourable exceptions believed, in their sudden blinding conversion and enthusiasm for the dry fly, that this had happened exclusively and entirely on the chalkstreams of Hampshire and that throughout the rest of the country everyone naturally fished the wet fly, the sunk fly, and mostly downstream.

If only someone had experimented with a horse-hair line at that time they would have had to modify their beliefs to a very great extent. Most of the progress in fly design and presentation had been made not on the chalkstreams but on the limestone and spate rivers of the midlands and the north of England and the Scottish Borders.

But now, perhaps with a sideways glance at the curious history of Kelson and the salmon fly and the birth of angling on the reservoirs, we come to the revolutionary inventions of the Americans which allowed flyfishing to burst through its previous limited frontiers to explore deep-water territories which hitherto could only have been reached by bait and spinner.

This was the space age revolution of plastic lines and graphite rods which began in the 1950s and is set to continue to provide flyfishers with tackle and flies of a sophistication that not even our fathers could have imagined possible.

Yet with all our progress in fly design, in presentation of the fly and in rivercraft, the basic principles of flyfishing remain as they were two thousand years ago. It is still to present to the fish a flicker of life in the water which gives the impression of something they may be tempted to eat, a kind of conjuring trick, the creation of an illusion.

There are no rules, no certainties. One relies on:

> that craft of the wilderness, that facility of appreciating the ways of bird and beast and fish and insect, the acquirement of which was, through countless centuries, the one great primary interest of primitive man.
>
> (J. W. Dunne, *Sunshine and the Dry Fly*, 1924)

Conrad Voss Bark
Lifton, Devon

CHAPTER ONE

The Macedonian Method

Flyfishing began at least two thousand years ago. Possibly more. It began because it was the best way of catching fish that were feeding on the surface on winged insects, the caddis or sedge flies, mayflies, olives, upwinged flies, black gnats, whatever names they had for them. The names would have been different. The flies were the same. So were the trout.

With the big flies whose bodies were more than an inch long there would have been no problem. They could be caught and impaled on a hook then dapped amid the rising fish. The big stone fly would have been admirable for dapping.

But there were other flies, smaller, more delicate, whose bodies would break if they were pierced by a hook. There would have been times in those far off days as there are now when trout would feed selectively on particular kinds of small surface insects and ignore subaqueous food while they were doing so. It would have infuriated an angler to see trout feeding avidly on small flies hatching on the surface while ignoring his worm.

We know from the writings of Homer and others that anglers were skilled in the ways of nature and the habits of fish. They were used to creating artificial lures such as plumes - we would call them streamer flies - and had fished them for thousands of years. They made them from feathers of the sea mew (seagull) tied to a hook that had been wrapped in wool of

1

a Laconian red. We are not certain what colour Laconian red would have been but the likelihood is a bright scarlet. The Romans used these plumes to take salmon from the rivers of Gaul and also from the Thames and Tyne when they came to

Seventh century BC version of the float tube

England. Making artificial lures to catch fish was nothing new. Indeed there are suggestions that they go back three or four thousand years or more to the ancient Egyptian dynasties. The Chinese are said to have used a kingfisher's feather as a hook bait several thousand years BC but we know no more than that. Possibly that too would have been a plume, a streamer.

But to use feathers to suggest a winged insect was a more complicated matter. So far as we know the ancient Greeks, the people of Macedon, were the first to manage it. They used coloured wools for the body of the fly and for the wings mounted two cock's feathers on the hook which they took from a cock's cape, as we do today.

We have a description of the Macedonian method from Aelian, a Spanish writer living in Rome, who seems to have made his living from what we might now call popular journalism. He lived from about 170 to 230 AD and wrote about the marvels of nature, some of which he had heard of from others and not actually seen for himself. Flyfishing was one.

We have the details, such as they are, from his book *De Natura Animalium* which was probably dated about 200 AD. The reference to flyfishing is brief and is given here as translated by Lambert in Radcliffe's *Fishing from the Earliest Times*:

> I have heard of a Macedonian way of catching fish and it is this: between Bercea and Thessalonica runs a river called the Aestraeus and in it there are fish with speckled skins; what the natives of the country call them you had better ask the Macedonians. These fish feed on a fly peculiar to the country which hovers on the river. It is not like flies found elsewhere nor does it resemble a wasp in appearance, nor in shape would one justly describe it as a midge or a bee; yet it has something of each of these, it imitates the colour of a wasp and it hums like a bee. The natives generally call it the hippourus.

Aelian flounders when he tries to describe the fly. It does not sound like any fly known to us or for that matter to the Macedonians. However, he then goes on to say the flies are so delicate they cannot be put on the hook to use as bait. So the fishermen's cunning comes into play:

> ...they have planned a snare for the fish and get the better of them by their fishermen's craft. They fasten red wool round a hook and fix on to the wool two feathers which grow under a cock's wattles and which in colour are like wax. Their rod is six feet long and their line of the same length. Then they throw their snare, and the fish, maddened and excited by the colour, come straight at it, thinking by the sight to get a dainty mouthful; when, however, it opens its jaws, it is caught by the hook and enjoys a bitter repast, a captive.

3

The flies that were the colour of unrefined wax were probably dun coloured. A six foot rod and line (if Aelian is correct) suggests dapping. The smallest Graeco-Roman hooks would be about 10 or 12 (Redditch scale). Flyfishing does not seem to have survived on the Aestraeus today, at least not in its original form:

> The river Aestraeus in Macedon is now known as the Kotichas. It is now a small river passing through the villages of Arkohorio and Monospita. Some rather unimportant species of fish can be found in the flatlands of Monospita...[but] in the mountainous area of Arkohorio there is trout fishing. Two methods of fishing are normally used, casting nets or using rods with either a dummy fish bait or a plume.
>
> (Greek Embassy spokesman)

After Aelian's description of flyfishing there is a gap. We know little or nothing of flyfishing for over a thousand years. There are hints here and there which might be about the fly but might also be about bait.

Around 900 AD an Abbot Aelfric, in Dorset or Devon, was said to have taught his pupils Latin by having a Latin translation placed underneath each Anglo-Saxon line of a text about fishing.

In France, around 1000 AD, a paper describing what has been said to have been flyfishing was written at the Abbey of St Bertin, near Omer, but it is believed to have been destroyed in one of the many wars which have ravaged that part of the world.

We assume, rightly or wrongly, that the knowledge of flyfishing came to Britain at about the time of the Norman invasion in 1066 but there is no hard evidence of this. The Norman knights were keen on manly sports, hunting and hawking, and one of the main sporting books in France at that time was *The Master of Game*, but it missed out flyfishing.

There is a manuscript version of *The Master of Game* translated into English probably around 1405 by Edward Duke of York who died in battle at Agincourt some ten years later. Sometime in the mid 1400s an unknown author added a fourth section to *The Master of Game* which dealt with flyfishing . A copy is in the Yale University Library. This script formed the basis of the first printed book in English about flyfishing which was produced at Caxton's press in Westminster in 1496 by Caxton's successor, Wynkyn de Worde, *The Treatyse of Fysshynge Wyth an Angle*.

The author of the *Treatyse* is traditionally supposed to have been a lady, a Dame Juliana Barnes or Berners, a lady of high birth who was prioress of Sopwell Priory near St Albans and the book was said to have been published at St Albans city.

Not so. An antiquarian, Jack Heddon, going through the Westminster Abbey archives some years ago found that the abbey's own researchers looking for the site of Caxton's press found that it was close to a house called St Albans. This was in the area now covered by grass to the east of the abbey's Chapter House where the statue of King George V now stands.

The colophon (printer's imprint) on the *Treatyse* - 'apud villa sancti Albani' - therefore meant near St Alban's house and was nothing to do with the city or abbey of St Albans. The confusion had arisen because Dame Juliana Barnes or Berners had been given as the author of the *Treatyse* on hunting, so it was assumed she had written the fishing treatyse as well.

Wynkyn de Worde didn't give it any specific by-line and the assumption was simply made that the same author had done both the hunting and the fishing treatises. But that was a hasty assumption as careful reading of both the treatises soon gives reason to suspect. The hunting one is full of admonitions of the

5

order of 'listen to your dame' whereas not one word of the fishing treatise makes even oblique reference to the author's gender. It could just as well have been written by a man.

(Arnold Gingrich, *The Fishing in Print*, 1974)

Even so it seems rather sad to abandon Berners after she had been regarded as the author of the book on fishing for nearly five hundred years. Waller Hills, in his *A History of Fishing for Trout*, says he does not like quoting an anonymous writer. I have a fellow feeling for him. Let us keep Berners as a matter of convenience.

So Berners' therefore is the first printed book in English on fishing, most of it on bait fishing - the majority interest - but it is a good account of flyfishing as well.

Some interpretation is necessary. The title itself, *Fysshynge Wyth an Angle*, means fishing with a hook, from the Anglo-Saxon word 'angul', a hook. Much of the writing is to our way of thinking tedious. Berners writes with fervour about how fishing improves the health of the body and how it is good for the soul, how you can say your prayers by the river, and how you should behave in a way that meets the approval of God and St Peter. The book seems to have been written for a leisured and sophisticated class so possibly Wynkyn de Worde, who might well have been editor as well as publisher was thinking of a readership largely in London.

London was still small, about the size of the walled city and it would not have taken men long to reach clean rivers. The Cray and the Wandle were chalkstreams and until Victorian times held a good stock of trout. There was the Westbourne brook (now underground to feed the Serpentine) and Holburn and Tyburn took their names from streams, and of course there was the Lea and the Fleet, and some of those held salmon as well as the Thames.

Berners gives detailed instructions how to make a rod that

6

would do for both bait and flyfishing. It had a butt made from willow or rowan. The butt was hollow (the pith was burnt out) and inside were carried the two top sections, made from other woods, and these would be taken out at the side of the river and spliced together, making a rod of about twelve to eighteen feet long. Bait fishermen could use such a rod as we use a modern roach pole.

It is quite possible that if a fisherman was not able to make such a rod then a master craftsman might do it for him. Berners went into the detail that a craftsman would need. Waller Hills, in his *History of Fishing for Trout*, was very impressed by the instructions:

> The casual reader, mislead by the archaic English in which the Treatyse is written, and above all by some of the clumsy plates [woodcuts] with which it is embellished, especially the frontispiece and that of the rod, may think that the practical part of the book is worthless. This is quite untrue: the rod, which in the picture looks like an ungainly pole, is really light and flexible: a hollow butt, a springy middle joint of hazel and a light yet tough top make up something which would throw a fly uncommonly well.

A master craftsman perhaps in Cheapside, and a member of a craft guild, with apprentices and journeymen attached to the workshop and living in, might have been prepared to burn out the pith from a rowan branch, ferrule the ends, fit a spike so the rod could be kept upright on the bank rather than laid down for people to walk over, and make all sound for gentlemen who could indulge in country sports.

It is also possible that merchants could supply tapered and twisted horsehair lines, twelve, fourteen or eighteen feet long, with the various links of horsehair - white would be the strongest - joined together by a water knot, tapered from ten hairs at the butt to two at the point. But this is speculation and whether the rod would come with the line attached is doubtful. It might have been outside the scope of the guild.

As an experiment some years ago, I made a Berners-type rod from a roach pole and parts of old cane rods. That was comparatively easy but the difficulty was making a horsehair line. It took several days to find the willing horse and several more to twist or plait a tapered line. Eventually I had a rod about 16-foot long and a line of about the same length tapered from something like twelve or fourteen hairs at the butt to three at the point. The butt was glued to a small leather bootlace which was glued and then whipped to the top of the rod. The master craftsman of Cheapside would have shuddered at the sight but it worked.

I could cast the horsehair line not only across the wind but against it, providing the wind was not too strong, which experts had told me was impossible with hair lines. It wasn't impossible at all.

Accompanied by two rather mystified dogs I took this enormous pole to a lake and made a cast. I had a small loch fly on the point, about a size 10, and it turned over well, sinking a little below the surface film and there, surprisingly, it stayed. What I had not realised and what the experts had not told me was that a hair line cannot sink. The fly did not have sufficient weight to pull it down. It remained visible in or just under the surface film. In modern parlance it was behaving like an emerger.

I jiggled the line. I tried to make the fly sink but it did not. I went from the lake to the river which was fairly close by and as I walked I did some false casting to dry the fly, which was the obvious thing to do and I suspect what Berners would have done if she had thought of mentioning it.

The river was small, rather well bushed, but with an open

space between the branches. I held the rod up, let the line blow out over the water, and let the fly touch the surface. Then I lowered the rod and allowed the fly to drift downstream. It drifted for about four or five feet and for half that distance it floated on the top of the water - it looked like a dry fly - and for the rest of the distance it assumed its natural role as an emerger. As I was doing this I suddenly remembered that this was how Izaak Walton had recommended us to fish. 'Let your fly only touch the water' he said, and that was what I had been doing for the first part of the drift. It felt odd in some strange way to think I was fishing as Walton would have told me.

Then I tried long casting, across the current, and this time the speed with which the fly landed put it below the surface of the water at once but again it did not sink any distance below the surface for the line was holding it up. Casting upstream was the same, though if I did one or two false casts - our ancestors called them whipping the line - then the fly would alight on the surface of the water, quite visible, and float for perhaps a foot or so before becoming waterlogged.

I had not expected the elasticity of horsehair. When I tried to break the fly off from three-strands of twisted horsehair it required a considerable pull. The hair link stretched for what seemed like several inches. I could now understand how fishermen could land quite a sizeable trout on a single hair.

But the greatest surprise of all was that the flies would not sink. This explains why our ancestors never bothered to talk about dry fly or wet fly fishing. There was no need. Their flies did both. You could dap them on the surface, as Izaak Walton said, or you could let them float for a short time with the line floating after them until they became waterlogged. You could also cast as far as you could and let the fly sink just below the surface, like an emerger.

In no way could our ancestors have fished the wet fly as

we can today, across and down, sinking several inches, perhaps a foot, below the surface. I tried fishing across and down myself and the fly, held up by the horsehair, became a wake fly, making a ruffle across the top of the water as it swung round.

No question about it. Our ancestors were attempting, within the limits of their technology, to fish their artificial flies on the surface of the water where the natural flies were hatching. They were attempting to fish a floating fly, what we would now call a dry fly, and when it sank, as it frequently did, they could fish it as an emerger pattern, or they could lift it off the water, whisk it dry and cast again. No wonder they did not discriminate between wet fly and dry. They could fish either one or the other in the same or in consecutive casts.

CHAPTER TWO

Wyngis of the Pertryche

B erners' advice to anglers is comparatively modern. In many
ways we have not changed a great deal in five hundred
years. It is true that every now and then she invokes God and St
Peter and tells readers to be good and say their prayers but that
was the fashion of the time. Berners was very firm on how to
behave:

> I charge you that you break no man's hedges in going about
> your sports, nor open any man's gates without shutting them
> again... Also you must not use this arteful sport for
> covetousness, merely for the increasing or saving of your
> money, but mainly for your enjoyment and to procure the health
> of your body and more especially of your soul.

A direct prohibition on selling your catch is far stronger than
modern angling codes which urge that anglers should merely be
discouraged from doing so. Moreover, anglers must avoid the
killer instinct:

> Also, you must not be too greedy in catching your said game
> [fish] as in taking too much at one time, a thing that can easily
> happen if you do in every point as this treatyse shows you. That
> could easily be the occasion of destroying your sport and other
> men's also. When you have a sufficient mess [catch] you should
> covet no more at that time.

All noble men must be concerned to protect the rivers and the fish:

> ...you must busy yourself to nourish the game in everything that you can, and to destroy all such things as are the devourers of it. And all these that do according to this rule will have the blessing of God and St Peter. That blessing may he grant who bought us with his precious blood.

All these quotations are from John McDonald's version of the *Treatyse* (see p.148) which uses modern words where the early-English might be confusing.

One of the problems about Berners is the dressings of the flies which are given in the text. Consider how clear and detailed are the instructions on rod making. They are quite precise. The master craftsman of Cheapside would know precisely what to do to make a rod, even if he had never or rarely seen a fishing rod before. But nothing of the kind applies to flies, what they represent or how they should be tied. This, for example, is the fly to be used in March:

> The dunne fly, the body of the donne woll, and the wyngis of the pertryche.

In modern English: the dun fly, the body of dun wool, and the wings of the partridge. That is all. Nothing more. What kind of partridge feathers, from the primary or secondary feathers of the wing, or the cape? Nothing is explained. Even the Macedonians, a thousand years before, were more precise.

This complete lack of information could be caused because the readers of the *Treatyse* would already know how to dress a partridge fly, so there was no need to tell them, which is unlikely, or because the flies were so easily obtained from tackle shops in Westminster and London that the author did not bother to explain how they should be tied. The third possibility is that the author did not know.

The third is the most likely. The theory is that the *Treatyse*, in publishing language, is a scissors and paste job. The unknown author - let us still call him or her Berners - was

but that pe ihptte thepin agapn. ¶ Alſo pe ſhall not vſe this for ſapd raſtp dpſporte for no couetpſenes to thenⱴreaſpnge ⱬ ſpa rpnge of pour monep oonlp but prpncppallp for pour ſolace ⱬ to cauſe the helthe of pour bodp.and ſperpallp of pour ſoule . ffor Whanne pe purpoos to goo on pour diſportes in fpſſhpng pe Woll not deſpre grerlp manp perſones Wpth pou.Whiche mp ghte lette pou of pour game.And thenne pe mape ſerue god de uoWtlp in ſapenge affectuouſlp poure cuſtumable praper. And thus dopnge pe ſhall eſcheWe ⱬ vopde manp vices.as poplnes Whpche is prpncppall cauſe to endure man to manp other vp ⸗ res.as it is rpght Well knoWen. ¶ Alſo pe ſhall not be to raueno us in takpng of pour ſapd game as to moche at one tpme: Whi

Extract from Juliana Berners' Treatyse

called in by the printer, Wynkyn de Worde, given one of the earlier manuscripts of the *Treatyse*, and told to produce an up-to-date version. Even more likely is that de Worde took the early written manuscript himself and printed the whole thing just as he found it. Perhaps the technique of dressing flies was defaced, or lost, or was not mentioned. We do not know.

What kind of a fly was the partridge? It is not clear. Modern writers differ. Lawrie and Skues think it must be a March Brown while Waller Hills suggests a February Red. I would have thought that the March Brown was more likely but it is difficult to say. If it is the March Brown then this fly is known in northern France and in some parts of England and Wales but not in rivers in southern England. Does this suggest a Norman origin of the original manuscript?

13

There is no doubt however that all of the twelve flies given in the *Treatyse* are suggestions or imitations of winged insects that would normally be found on the surface of the water. Some we can recognise. The stone fly for example. Others are doubtful. There is a sedge and a mayfly. Berners knew something of entomology.

The book itself must have been aimed at the London market, the sophisticated members of the great merchant companies, mercers, grocers, drapers, fishmongers, goldsmiths, the merchant aristocrats who ruled the capital, the lawyers of the inns of court, the merchant venturers, wool merchants and many others, for London, even during the troubles of the Wars of the Roses, was a peaceful city with a growing and prosperous middle class. It was, as the Scottish poet Dunbar said, 'the flower of cities all'.

And London was fortunate because it was simply surrounded by rivers. The Thames was pure and clear above the stews and drains of the city. The salmon could not be fished legally as the fishing rights were held by the Fishmonger's Company. But the river was full of roach and perch and dace. There were great shoals of dace at Westminster. The river Wandle which flowed into the Thames by the village of Wandsworth was a chalkstream and full of trout.

We have no account of fishermen of that time except one, a bait fisherman, probably an apprentice, who was walking through the city streets at some early hour in the morning and was arrested as a vagrant by the watch and brought before the magistrates at Guildhall. He was asked to explain what he was doing at that time in the morning and he replied: 'Sir, I am a roach fisher and I was on my way to the river'. The magistrate dismissed the case with the comment that 'roach fishers were all honest men'.

The *Treatyse* must have been well received. There were

many reprintings, and it was pirated by writers and publishers over the next two hundred years. Some of the *Treatyse* flies, in some cases hardly recognisable, appeared in the first edition of Izaak Walton's *Compleat Angler* in 1653. Walton was no fly fisher and took the information from Thomas Barker, the chef to Lord Montague.

Title page of the Treatyse

Berners mentions salmon but briefly, merely that 'salmon do rise to the fly but it is seldom seen'. There are no special instructions for fishing for them. Salmon were protected by law and had been ever since the Romans had established netting

15

stations on the Seine estuary in France and on Severn, Thames and Tyne. One suspects that legionaires would have fished for them on their time off from depot duty. Radcliffe reports a mosiac showing a man with a pointed cap fishing with a rod and a line, presumably a Roman soldier, which was discovered at Lydney in Gloucestershire, an area connected with the river Severn salmon fishery (see p 147). The Romans used artificial minnows and plumes for rod and line fishing. The minnows were made from slightly curved cow horn with a hook attached, in shape something like the modern Toby or kidney spoons. Their feathered lures - plumes - were rather like the 'feathers' which Cornish boatmen use for mackerel fishing. The Romans would use them not only for sea fishing but for estuaries and rivers.

But basically, salmon fishing was a commercial business and the fish were netted on a large scale. Dried and pickled salmon were used to feed the troops in many of the wars of the Middle Ages and earlier. Edward II (1284 -1327) ordered 3,000 dried salmon for one of his campaigns. Sport fishing for salmon was still some way off. But for trout fishing, especially with the fly, Berners had set the scene and provided the inspiration that was to last with very few changes for the next hundred and fifty years.

CHAPTER THREE

Cromwell's General

The first efforts to improve the art of flyfishing, particularly the more sophisticated design of artificial flies, had to wait more or less for the time of the Civil War in the middle of the 17th Century. This was really very strange for it was a century of bitter religious intolerance, persecution, burnings of heretics and conflict between king and parliament which set father against son and brother against brother. Yet in spite of all this more fishing books were published during these times than ever before and more people were going fishing. One of our great historians, G. M. Trevelyan, sums up the paradox:

> Fortunately most of the common people who kept the sheep in Shakespeare's countryside, or wandered by Izaak Walton's streams, fishing rod in hand, were untroubled by Bunyan's and Cromwell's visions of heaven and hell; but saint and sinner, happy fisherman and self-torturing fanatic, all were subject to the wholesome influence of that time and landscape.

Many men must have turned away from the horrors of civil war towards the river bank, among them an ironmonger and haberdasher in Fleet Street, Izaak Walton, a royalist who feared for his life, who fled London to Winchester, and in peace and tranquillity and in old age wrote a book that has gained him immortality. *The Compleat Angler*, a story of Arcady, is a book

17

for all time but Walton was not a flyfisherman and it is to two of his contemporaries that we must turn.

The man who had the greatest influence at this time on the development of flyfishing was Robert Venables, one of

Robert Venables, the Cromwellian soldier

Cromwell's leading generals. He fought in England and in Ireland and was in charge of an ill-fated Cromwellian expedition to the West Indies. The expedition had not turned out as Cromwell hoped so Venables was put into the Tower of

London without trial and kept there for a long time, quite how long is uncertain. It was there that Venables spent many days writing his fishing book, *The Experienced Angler*, which was published in 1662.

Venables is far less known than Charles Cotton of Dovedale who wrote the second part of *The Compleat Angler* for Walton. Cotton basked in Walton's glory and also produced a whole series of new fly dressings which have filled the anthologies. Lawrie (*A Reference Book of English Trout Flies*) quotes Cotton at length but does not mention Venables because Cotton gave a list of 65 named trout flies and Venables did not give one.

The whole purpose of Venables' book was very different. There is a good biographical sketch of him by C.G.A. Parker in the Antrobus Press edition of *The Experienced Angler* which was published in 1969 and provides valuable background to the uncertainties and agonies of a soldier's life under Cromwell. The Venables family had held land in Cheshire since the Norman invasion. In 1642 on the outbreak of the Civil War Venables raised 'a company of foot in Lancashire, determined that Parliament and not the King should predominate'. He fought well and was at the taking of Chester and was probably there at the time that Charles I was executed in Whitehall. Parker comments:

> The regicide divided the loyalties of the English for decades to come and it profoundly affected the course of Venables' life in future years.

After holding several important posts, Venables was sent to Ireland where he took part in the seige of Drogheda and the butchery of civilians which followed. Venables was then sent to Ulster as commander-in-chief. The local population's hatred of Cromwell and their loyalty to the crown must have added to the doubts in his mind. Nevertheless Venables played a leading part in reducing Ireland to submission. Parker again:

> Fortunately for him he could go fishing and in his own words 'pursue that recreation which composeth the soul to that calmness and serenity which gives a man the possession and fruition of himself and all his enjoyments'.

By now it was more than probable that Venables had developed royalist sympathies. All the same he accepted command as general of an expeditionary force to invade Spanish territory in the West Indies. Reinforced by more men, Venables captured Jamaica, but was defeated in attempts to take Hispaniola, partly from illness, partly because of a split command, and partly because although he was a good regimental commander he might not have been a great enough general to command an army of 9,000 men. On his return to London he faced Cromwell's anger, was interned in the Tower without trial and his commands and rank were taken from him. But the person who was really to blame was probably Cromwell, for the expedition had been badly planned from the the beginning.

Venables, an arrogant man with a great and a justified opinion of himself as a soldier, was resentful at the way he had been treated. After his release he retired with his wife to Cheshire, raised a force for the Royalist cause, was defeated and escaped, but on the Restoration was appointed governor of Chester Castle.

In his old age, Venables was rather a bitter man who quarrelled with his family. A sad story, typical of many personal tragedies of the civil war. Perhaps it was some consolation that his book, with a foreword by Izaak Walton, was a success, went into five editions and had pride of place in many booksellers and tackle shops, such as Walton's favourite shop where he bought tackle, The Three Trouts in St Paul's

Churchyard. I daresay too it was taken by stage coach from the George Inn at Aldersgate to shops in Winchester and Salisbury. Delivery would take two days.

Fishing had become popular. Rods, lines, creels, landing nets and flies, even the newly-invented reels, could be bought in many shops and Walton's praise for Venables would have helped sales. His letter to Venables had the same kindness, courtesy and charm which characterised him throughout his life. 'Honoured Sir', he began:

> Though I never to my knowledge had the happiness to see your face, yet accidentally coming to a view of this discourse before it went to the press; I held myself obliged in point of gratitude for the great advantage I received thereby, to tender you my particular acknowledgement, especially having been for thirty years past, not only a lover but a practiser of that innocent recreation, wherein by your judicious precepts I find myself fitted for a higher form; which expression I take the boldness to use, because I have read and practised by many books of this kind, formerly made public; from which though I received much advantage in the practice, yet without prejudice to their worthy authors, I could never find in them that height of judgment and reason which you have manifested in this, as I may call it, epitome of Angling.

It was a pretty good introduction to the book and remember again that this is a confirmed royalist, who must have been aware of Venables' record, who deliberately set out without any prompting to pay tribute to a man whose political and possibly religious opinions he would hold in contempt.

Put yourself in Walton's place. There was no advantage, possibly even the reverse, in writing such a letter to a man he did not know but, being the generous-minded man he was, there was no hesitation in crossing the boundary between two

21

opposing worlds.

So, what had prompted this remarkable letter? It was the quality of the book. Walton says he had read other books : Barker (1651) of course and probably Mascall (1590), Taverner (1600), Dennys (1606), Markham (1614) and others, and yet when you go through them they do not, efficient though they are, evoke any warmth, any emotional response of the kind or of the degree which you find in Venables. He was a most mature writer, as mature and well balanced as Berners had been.

Robert Venables starts his book with a discourse of the pleasures of angling which had been the sport of recreation of God's saints and many holy fathers 'both dead and at this time breathing'. So far he is with Berners, but his tackle is improved; a cane rod with a tapered horsehair line thick at the butt which will enable the angler to cast the fly better than a line which has only a modest taper. But after a brief preliminary introduction to rod, line and tackle he starts, as no other book has before him, with flyfishing.

Straightaway he dispenses with the Berners' theory that the natural flies and their imitations must be assigned to individual months of the season for 'scarce any one sort of fly doth continue its colour and virtue [for] one month'.

He discusses what fish will rise to a fly. They include salmon, trout, grayling, bleak, chevin, chub, roach and dace and though some angle with a fly for bream and pike 'I judge the labour lost and the knowledge a needless curiosity'. Then he gave the essence of flyfishing in a way that no one had done before, briefly and succintly summing up the dry fly, emerger and wet fly in this remarkable passage:

All the aforementioned sorts of fish [salmon, trout, grayling, etc] will sometimes take the Flie much better at the top of the

water, and at another time much better a little under the
superficies of the water, and in this your own observation must
be your constant and daily instructor (for if they will not rise to
the top try them under) it not being possible (in my opinion) to
give any certain rule in this particular...

So said Skues in his arguments with Halford on the dry fly two
hundred years later. The more one reads Venables the more
modern he appears. Now he goes on to discuss the habits of
water flies:

You may also observe (which my own experience taught me)
that Fish never rise eagerly and freely at any sort of Flie until
that kind come to the waters side; for though I often have at the
first coming in of some Flies (which I judged they loved best)
gotten several of them, yet I could never find they did much (if
at all) to value them, until those sorts of Flies began to flock to
the Rivers side, and were to be found on the trees and bushes
there in great numbers...

He advises fisherman on coming to the river to beat the boughs
of bushes to see what flies are there, and if there are several
kinds then 'try them all'. Sometimes the fish feed at different
times of the day, and after that they change again to other flies.

He does not know where the natural fly comes from nor
does he make a guess, like Walton, who thought they were bred
of the dew or of putrefaction. But he does know about the
spinner - 'of some kinds there are a second sort afterwards' -
and for these he suggests an 'orange fly'. That must be similar
to Skues' discovery that there are times when an Orange Quill
will be taken for the blue-winged olive spinner.

The natural fly must be copied by the artificial and
Venables gives detailed instructions, suggesting that the flies
should be tied to float with the point of the hook upwards on
the water:

> ... if I turn the feathers round the hook, then I clip away those that are on the back of the hook that so (if it be possible) the point of the hook may be forced by the feathers (left on the inside of the hook) to swim upwards; and by this means I conceive that the stream will carry your Flies wings in the posture of one flying; whereas if you set the points of the wings backwards towards the bending of the hook, the stream (if the feathers be gentle as they ought) will fold the points of the wings in the bending of the hook, as I have often found by experience.

This way of tying the fly was repeated in later years, was forgotten, and then reinvented with modification at some time in the early 1900s, around 1910.

The horsehair line for flyfishing must be twice the length of the rod, if the river is not too bushed, and the fly must be kept in continual motion, that is to say the angler would fish with the wind and dap the fly on the surface where it would dance up and down. He would also at times use hooks with a weight of fine lead on the shank and over this lead would tie chamois leather (shammy) for the body of a 'cadbait' (caddis pupa) with a black silk head for bottom fishing.

For slow rivers and stillwaters he uses a technique which is almost the same as nymph fishing. Cast the fly across the river and let it sink a little in the water:

> and draw him gently back again so as you break not the water, or raise any circles or motion in the water, and let the current of the River carry the flie gently down with the stream.

He pays little attention to the salmon:

> I must only add that salmon flies must be made with Wings standing one behind the other, whether two or four; also he [the salmon] delights in the most gaudy and orient colours you can

choose; the Wings I mean chiefly, if not altogether, with long tails and wings.

Venables is the forerunner of many of our own techniques. He experiments with fly dressings, insists on exact imitation of the

Title page of The Experienced Angler

natural insect, uses imitation bait with a fly rod. His dressing of the weighted caddis pupa is not all that different from the reservoir style of two hundred and fifty years later. He draws his fly under water without disturbing the surface film in the same way as a nymph fisherman and he insists that you must know whether the fish are taking the fly on the surface of the water or - that charming phrase - a little under the superficies of the water, and must act accordingly.

He uses a 'winch' (reel), a stronger rod and a running line of shoemaker's thread, with a ring at the top of the rod, for trolling for pike, but prefers a slender rod and the fixed horsehair line for the trout.

Venables was the first of the moderns. He discarded Berners. He described in great detail how the fly should be fished. His approach and his attitude survive to this day. Yet he has been neglected by some authors, mostly those who have been concerned, like Lawrie, purely with the fly dressings themselves. Venables gave advice on flies but did not provide patterns. The royalist, Charles Cotton, made no such mistake.

CHAPTER FOUR

Cotton, Walton and Barker

The hundred years from about 1590 onwards until the time of Venables and Cotton showed a slow but steady development of flyfishing, not only in new tackle - the introduction of whole cane rods, running lines and reels - but in a small but significant change of atmosphere and mood. The habits of natural flies and the ways of fish began to be studied more closely from a spirit of enquiry which had not been evident much before.

John Taverner, a surveyor of woodlands south of the Trent for King James I, published a book in 1600 with the rather long title of *Certaine Experiments Concerning Fish and Fruite* which describes the hatch of a fly from the nymph, though he calls them both a fly. Here it is, from the text quoted by Waller Hills:

> I have seen a young flie swimme in the water too and fro, and in the end come to the upper crust of the water, and assay to flie up: Howbeit not being perfitly ripe or fledge, hath twice or thrice fallen downe againe into the water; howbeit in the end receiving perfection by the heate of the sunne, and the pleasant fat water, hath in the end within some halfe houre after taken her flighte, and flied quite away into the aire. And of such young flies before they are

able to flie awaie do fish feede exceedingly.

Men began to observe the natural world more closely. They brooded on what they saw and became fascinated by it. It was a slow progress, it took time, but here and there they started to watch, to ask questions, and to try and find the answers. It would be wrong to say that the starting point of our knowledge of the natural fly began with an examination by a surveyor of woodlands into the remarkable things that he saw around him but certainly Taverner would have been a help. Other books from other writers followed: on husbandry, fish ponds, fish breeding and entomology.

One fly fisher who began to study insect life was an aristocrat, Charles Cotton (1630-1687) who had an estate on the Dove, a lovely limestone trout stream on the borders of Staffordshire and Derbyshire. His work is remembered because of his association with Izaak Walton.

Walton (1593-1683) was a bait fisher and knew nothing about flyfishing so in his first edition of *The Compleat Angler* (1653) the flyfishing section was taken from a book published two years earlier, Barker's *Art of Angling* (1651).

Walton was a literary man as well a shopkeeper and wrote biographies of Sir Henry Wotton and John Donne. He was near to sixty and had retired to Winchester when he wrote *The Compleat Angler*, and possibly he wrote it because he was lonely. His two wives and seven of his eight children were dead. So also were two close friends and fishing companions.

He wrote of past happiness, of good companions, singing milkmaids, happy shepherds and idyllic fishing parties in sylvan surroundings. It was a picture of old England, of a world of romance, which in Britain alone has been republished more than a hundred times and, world wide, some 400 editions in 60 languages. No wonder his friend Cotton wanted to write a new section at the end of the book on flyfishing to make up for the

Charles Cotton, who wrote the flyfishing section of the fifth edition of The Compleat Angler for his friend Isaak Walton

brief and inadequate references to the fly in the first edition. His text, attempting to follow Walton's style, was added to the fifth edition of *The Compleat Angler* in 1676, some 23 years after the book was first published.

We do not know how Walton and Cotton met. Both were royalists. Walton's book had been written during the Civil War and during Cromwell's dictatorship all royalists were still in danger. There may have been a family connection - Walton came from Stafford - but it is probable that Cotton wrote to Walton on the publication of Walton's first edition and invited him to come and stay.

Cotton was much younger than Walton and treated the older man with great deference and affection, calling him father, respecting his reputation as a biographer as well as a fisherman. Cotton was a poet and his works had been published so they had much in common. After the Restoration and the return of Charles II to the throne, Cotton was known as one of the Restoration poets with Sedley and the Earl of Rochester.

Cotton's addition to Walton's work did not in any way match the charm of *The Compleat Angler* although Cotton clearly made great efforts to follow Walton's style. However, Walton was unique and no one could possibly copy him. For this reason Cotton's script has frequently been dropped from a number of later editions of *The Compleat Angler* as being of only secondary interest so far as the general reader is concerned.

This is true. On one occasion it was also excluded by a prudish editor because Cotton, as one of the Restoration poets, had a reputation of being a licentious man. Apart from one or two poems that praised the delights of being a bachelor and having the pleasure of a number of ladies there is nothing particularly licentious about Cotton. He was married to a lady who died and after that he married again and he was as far as we know a reasonably happy married man.

Cotton's significance to flyfishermen is less as an angler, more as a fly dresser. In the second part of *The Compleat Angler* he gives a list of 65 fly patterns for trout and grayling and the months during the season when they should be used.

He abandoned the Berners dressings completely though Barker and Walton were still hanging on to them. He tells us about small flies which were probably midges; and he knew, which Walton did not, that many flies came from creatures that lived in the river and rose to the surface to hatch. Until Cotton the general impression was the same as that given by Walton, that flies were probably hatched from dew heated by the sun or from putrefaction. Cotton dispenses with all that.

He tells us quite frankly that most of the fish caught on the Dove were taken by just a few flies - various dressings of the Green Drake, the Grey Drake and the Stone Fly - but he simply cannot resist giving us dressings of a huge number of others, most of which we cannot identify, apparently for the sheer pleasure that a fly dresser has in his craft. I have no doubt that if Cotton was alive today he would have been chairman of a fly dressers' guild. Think of the work he put into this one dressing:

> The artificial green-drake...is made upon a large hook, the dubbing camel's hair, bright bear's hair, the soft down that is combed from a hog's bristles, and yellow camlet [wool or goat's hair], well mixed together; the body long, and ribbed about with green silk, or rather yellow, waxed with green wax; the whisks of the tail of the long hairs of sables or fitchet [polecat]; and the wings of the white-grey feather of a mallard, dyed yellow; which is also dyed thus: Take the root of a barbary tree, and shave it, and put to it woody viss, with as much alum as a walnut, and boil your feathers in it in rainwater; and they will be of a very fine yellow.

Most of the bait fishers of Cotton's time were very keen to anoint their worms or caddis grubs with magic potions to make them more attractive to the fish, such things as the marrow from the thigh bone of a heron, man's fat, or the powdered bones of a man's skull. Witchcraft and magic potions were common enough in the minds of people at that time so it would not be surprising if a fly dresser had not tried something of that kind on his flies but Cotton never got any further than clipping

The small leather creel inscribed with the initials 'I.W.', which is reputed to have belonged to Isaak Walton

the hair from the beard of a black cat for his dressing of the Grey Drake.

Other curious things for dubbing such as camel's and bear's hair might well have been obtained by mail order from London shops like The Three Trouts in St Pauls Churchyard, or from the haberdashery section of Walton's ironmonger's business in his shop four doors west of Chancery Lane in Fleet Street. Most of the other materials could have been got on Cotton's Beresford estate, probably collected by the same boy who used to accompany him on his fishing trips to carry the food and drink and net the fish.

Cotton's flies were pirated by subsequent writers, including James Chetham (*The Angler's Vade Mecum*, 1681) who introduced starling wings instead of mallard for his dressings but rather disgraced himself by anointing bait with graveyard materials pounded to a kind of unguent.

We learn very little from Chetham but a great deal from Cotton whose work was used and developed by many writers in the 18th and 19th centuries. You will notice, for example, that to get the right shade of green for the body ribbing in the Green Drake dressing he uses yellow silk that had been waxed with green wax. This is the same method used for the body of the fly for Canon Greenwell by James Wright in May, 1854 - yellow silk waxed to make it look green.

Cotton's patterns, some of his ideas, and some of the names of his flies - such as the Blue Dun - are still with us. Towards the end of his life he had heart trouble. He died in 1687 and is buried in what was then the new church of St James's, Westminster, which is now known as St James's Piccadilly. His poetry is forgotten but his flies are remembered: so is his advice to 'fish fine and far off'.

At this time men were fishing the fly for salmon in the Thames. They may well have been doing so for many years, way back into the early 1600s but we lack the evidence. It finally comes from Thomas Barker, the friend of Walton, who provided Walton with information on flyfishing which Walton included in his first edition of the *The Compleat Angler* in 1653, but the details about salmon fishing with the fly are best taken from Barker's own book, *Barker's Delight, or The Art of Angling*, which came out in 1651 two years before Walton.

Barker was a cook - these days we would call him a chef - at one of the aristocratic houses at Westminster not far away from Inigo Jones's royal banqueting hall in Whitehall. He was also an experienced angler and would go out to the landing stages or the beaches close to where Westminster Bridge now stands - there was a ferry in those days - and catch fish for Lord Montague's banquets.

Barker introduced his book - quite a small volume - with a charming modesty by saying he was 'not a scholler' but even so his narrative was clear and precise. There is a small section on salmon fishing and as this is the first detailed account we have it is worth quoting it fairly fully. The American writer J. D. Bates has put it into modern English:

I will now show you the way to take a salmon.

The first thing you must gain must be a rod of some ten foot in the stock, that will carry a top of six foot pretty stiff and strong, the reason is there must be a little wire ring at the upper end of the top for the line to run through, that you may take up and loose the line at your pleasure; you must have your winder within two foot of the bottom to go on your rod made in this manner, with a spring, that you may put it in as low as you please.

The salmon swimmeth most commonly in the midst of the river...[and] if you angle for him with a fly which he will rise to like a trout, the flie must be made of a large hook, which must carry six wings, or four at least; there is judgment in making those flies... You must be sure that you have your line of twenty six yards in length that you may have your convenient time to turn him; but if you turn him you are very like to have the fish with small tackles; the danger is all in the running out both of salmon and trout, you must forecast to turn the fish as you do a wild horse, either upon the right or left hand, and wind up in your line as you find occasion in guiding your fish to the shore, having a good large landing hook to take him up.

There it is, absolutely complete, down to the smallest detail: a running line for a fish that goes off like a wild horse when hooked and needs side strain to turn him and a gaff 'to take him up'. You could not ask for much more. There is no doubt that Barker is not only speaking of his own experience but of that which had been handed down to him from other anglers of time past. The only problem is the fly.

The plume of the Romans is discarded in favour of a fly with wings, a true fly, and this is most likely to follow the precedent in the *Treatyse* when salmon would, though not often, take an imitation of a winged fly intended for trout. The winged fly tradition continues but it became clear at some time, possibly in the early 1600s, that salmon needed a larger fly than those provided by Berners and one that had to be mounted on a large hook, larger than those used for trout.

The largest natural flies seen on the river were dragon and damsel flies and those the fly fishermen began to imitate, giving them several pairs of wings and a rather thick dubbed body for the dragon fly, a thinner body, probably bright blue, for the damsel fly.

They may well have known that these flies were, in the old phrase, 'born of the water', which links up with Taverner and his explanation of how a nymph turns into the sub-imago of the winged insect. We have no idea how Barker's artificials were

35

fished but I suspect they would be true wet flies and presented with a sinking line. The line - twenty six yards of it - was probably made of shoemaker's thread or hemp or wool, bought at The Three Trouts and soaked in oil to help prevent rotting. We do not know for certain but that seems to be the most likely explanation.

One can visualise Barker walking down to the Thames - possibly only a few yards - and wading out into the shallows. In those days there were no embankments and many boats would be beached, though the big barges had a landing stage, possibly several, on piers further out into the river. Beyond a certain point up river there would be free fishing, especially for those on the staff of the big houses.

Salmon were netted further down river, below London Bridge, and were brought in to the Billingsgate Market set up under a charter granted to the City of London by Edward III in 1327. They were served at banquets at Guildhall together with other fish that were brought in by trawl boats from deep sea fishing in the North Sea. Most of the fish especially in hot weather would have to be salted or kept in brine so that the arrival at the grace-and-favour houses in Whitehall of the cook carrying a fresh-caught salmon would be most welcome.

Altogether the seventeenth had been a remarkable century. Flyfishing had become more popular, there had been a new understanding of insect life, new patterns of trout flies, improvements in rods, the invention of the reel and the running line, the publication of more books on angling than ever before, and one of them, Walton's picture of pastoral England with singing milkmaids and honest anglers, was to become a classic worldwide; and then, at long last, the beginning of a salmon fly. It was a remarkable achievement.

CHAPTER FIVE

The Ludlow Doctor

It is probably true to say that modern fly fishing began and developed with the Stuarts, the Cromwellian period, and the Restoration. The rods and reels and lines were recognisably the same kind that were used up to the mid and late Victorian era. Many of Cotton's flies were prototypes of those we use today. From about the years 1600 to 1690, something like a dozen books on fishing were published containing much new information and advice. During that period there was a tremendous growth of invention.

Cane rods, though not *split* cane, made their appearance, ferrules, wicker creels, running lines, reels, new fly designs from the first serious entomological studies by Taverner (1600), Venables (1662), and Cotton (1676). Greater efforts were made to ensure that the flies floated better, one of the annoying habits of the Berners patterns.

New materials which were more buoyant, such as bear's hair, were used for bodies and William Lawson (1614) went so far as to fold slivers of cork 'cunningly about the hook' to get a better drift. It was, of course, an inventive century for in other spheres of discovery Newton was absorbed in gravity, Harvey with the circulation of the blood, and Halley with the arrival of a comet.

During this time we have the first detailed account of fishing for salmon in Scotland. One of Cromwell's commanders Colonel Richard Franck, left for Scotland just before Cromwell's death, possibly in order to avoid persecution which was prevalent at the time.

For whatever reason he spent a long time, possibly as much as year, touring most of Scotland from the Borders to Sutherland and fishing as he went. His *Northern Memoirs*, a travel book, was written about the time that Cromwell died (1658) but was not published for another 16 years.

Waller Hills says in his history that he cannot stand Franck, who was arrogant, boastful, fell out with Walton, could not write without using the most obscure and complicated language, and was wasting everyone's time with religious and political arguments. All this is true. Yet sometimes Franck was unconsciously funny, when for example, he came to Angus:

> where Scotland's great general, the Earl of Leven, was born promiscuously from obscure parents.

Franck started off on the Borders, going north, fishing the Annan and the Nith. He thought they were beautiful rivers. Then he went on to Glasgow, staying at an inn on the way where he had been 'worried to death by lice' so that his skin was 'all over mottled like an April trout'. Fishing the Clyde he caught both trout and a salmon.

He used a fly with a bear's hair body and a teal wing. On one occasion he was broken by a salmon about which he says:

> Be mindful therefore to throw him line enough if provided you purpose to seek his destruction.

He used a running line on a reel and a landing hook (a gaff) to land his salmon. He seemed to have no difficulty in finding places to fish for 'if you may practice where you please in any river in Scotland', as though he was pleasantly surprised to find freedom after his experiences in England. He passed through

'Dirty Dunblain' where he told the story of how a salmon leaps up a waterfall by taking its tail in its mouth and releasing it like 'a well-tempered spring'. He came to Stirling:

> where the Firth runs here that washeth and meets the foundations of the city; but relieves the country with her plenty of salmon; where the burgo masters as in many other parts of Scotland are compelled to reinforce an ancient statute that commands all masters and others not to force or compel any servant or an apprentice to feed on salmon more than thrice a week.

He fished usually downstream, dibbling the fly for trout, but he says very little about the fishing for he carries on imaginary conversations on religion and philosophy, mixed with rather doubtful local colour and unlikely stories. He says of the county of Ross that the earth there 'has an antipathy against rats'. He thought the Highlands

> represent a part of the creation left undrest; as some great and magnificent fabric is erected you know the abundance of rubbish is left to remove.

He went to Aberdeen to fish the Dee and down south to Edinburgh, and on to the Tweed. He says you need a swivel with the running line for salmon on the Tweed and describes the fly:

> The ground of your fly be for the most part obscure, of a gloomy dark and dusty complexion, fashioned with tufts of bear's hair, blackish or brownish discoloured wool, interwoven sometimes with peacock's feathers, at others lap'd about with grey, red, yellow, green or blewish silk, simple colours, or sometimes colours intermingled.

Not for another hundred years would the Scottish rivers see the brilliantly coloured salmon flies that came from Ireland.

Franck is probably best remembered for his argument with Walton about pike being born from the pickerel weed. Franck said it was nonsense and Walton did not like being criticised,

Northern Memoirs,

Calculated for the

Meridian of SCOTLAND.

Wherein moſt or all of the **Cities, Cita dels, Sea-ports, Caſtles, Forts, Fortreſſes, Rivers** and **Rivulets** are compendiouſly deſcribed.

Together with choice Collections of Various Diſcoveries, Remarkable Obſervations, Theological Notions, Political Axioms, National Intrigues, Polemick Inferences, Contemplations, Speculations, and ſeveral curious and induſtrious Inſpections, lineally drawn from Antiquaries, and other noted and intelligible Perſons of Honour and Eminency.

To which is added,

The Contemplative & Practical Angler, by way of Diverſion. With a Narrative of that dextrous and myſterious Art experimented in *England,* and perfected in more remote and ſolitary Parts of *Scotland.*

By way of Dialogue.

Writ in the Year 1658, but not till now made publick,

By **Richard Franck**, Philanthropus.

Plures necat Gula quam Gladius.

LONDON,
Printed for the Author. To be ſold by *Henry Mortclock* at the *Phenix,* in St. *Paul's* Church-yard. 1694.

Richard Franck's 'Memoir', written in 1658

especially by a Puritan. So they parted company. Franck was right but Walton refused to correct the passage about pickerel weed in his book.

It was a credulous age and Walton's *The Compleat Angler* is full of imaginary stories from so-called authorities. Walton was not alone in all this. James Chetham quoted (1681) a magical recipe that had come from an apothecary to a French king which consisted of a mixture of various herbs with 'man's fat, cat's fat and powdered mummy 'which if smeared for eight inches above the hook would compel fish to bite.

After the 17th century the mood changes. There was a pause in the publication of angling books, almost as though flyfishermen needed to brood and discuss the outpouring of ideas and inventions of the Walton and Cotton era. We are approaching the age of transition, the 1700s when, freed from the conflict of king and parliament, we see the beginnings of an industrial revolution and the great campaigns for liberty in the American colonies and in France. The historian G.M.Trevelyan says it was a classical age:

> That is to say an age of unchallenged assumption, when the philosophers of the street, such as Dr Johnson, have ample leisure to moralise on the human scene.

Fishermen too had more leisure in a more settled society. The increase in scientific knowledge was to lead to more practical judgments on fish and fly. This was the hallmark of a new generation of flyfishermen, again from the provinces, of whom the most significant was a doctor, Richard Bowlker, who had a practice in Ludlow, Shropshire, and who fished the Teme and the Severn.

Bowlker was the author of *The Art of Angling* published locally in or around 1747 during the reign of George II. It was a practical handbook which set the example of many that were to follow. After Richard Bowlker died the book was enlarged and practically rewritten by his son Charles, and several editions followed for a number of years.

Both the Bowlkers were aware of the new scientific papers which were being printed at various universities on subjects which affected fish and flies. This was the time of the foundation of the Royal Society at Burlington House in Piccadilly and the researches of the great Carl Linnaeus at the University of Upsala where he was professor of botany.

We do not know whether Richard Bowlker was a corresponding member of the Royal Society which might have given him access to a good deal of information, but it might have been so. He was well briefed on the life of the salmon, its habit of losing its appetite on the spawning run; he knew a great deal of the ways of water-bred flies, the nymph hatching into the sub-imago, and the transposition to the fully adult fly. He examined Charles Cotton's fly patterns and quite rightly discarded a number that were obscure. His own patterns were exceptionally good. This is his Blue Dun (the large dark olive):

> Comes down about the beginning of March and continues until the middle of April. His wings are made of the feather of the starling's wing, or the blue feathers that grow under the wing of a duck widgeon; the body is made of the blue fur of a fox, or the blue part of the squirrels fur, mixed with a little yellow mohair, and a blue cock's hackle wrapped over the body, in imitation of the legs: As he swims down the water his wings stand upright on his back; his tail forked and of the same colour as his wings. He appears on the water about ten o'clock in the forenoon, and continues until about three in the afternoon but the principal time of the day is from twelve till two; the flies then coming down in great quantities, and are always more plentiful in dark, cold, gloomy days than in bright sun-shine weather.

Title page of Brooke's Art of Angling

I am not sure whether it was the father or son who described a hatch of fly on the Teme but it gives some idea of the prolific hatches of fly before so many rivers were destroyed by factory effluent during the industrial revolution:

> it is amazing to see, in a moment's time, the surface of the water almost covered over with ten thousand of these pretty little flying insects, and the fish rising and sporting at them in so much you would think the whole river was alive.

So far as we know the Bowlkers mostly fished the Shropshire rivers. They knew London well for they spoke of the five tackle shops that they visited in the city. The gossiping that went on at these shops helped to spread the news of fish and fishing. We hear nothing about the Hampshire rivers though some of the Bowlker patterns would certainly have been most effective on the chalkstreams. His caddis fly had wings of buff-coloured hen feathers, the body of buff mohair warped with a pale yellow hackle on a 14 hook.

Although Bowlker knew that salmon were disinclined to eat in fresh water he imagined that when they showed on the surface they were rising to take dragon or damsel flies.

Therefore the flies that he dressed for salmon were suggestions or imitations of these large flies and this led to the creation of the glorious butterfly-hued artifical flies of McKay, O'Gorman, Rogan and Kelson in the years that followed. Bowlker had not heard of the Graeco-Roman plumes for salmon fishing and it is a nice speculation to know what might have happened if he had.

Here then are Bowlker's dressings of salmon flies. There may have been earlier dressings of this quality, possibly in Ireland, but if so there seems to be no printed record that survives. Bowlker's first dressing is of the Dragon Fly, also called Libella:

The wings are made of a reddish brown feather from the wing of the cock turkey, the body of auburn - coloured mohair warped with yellow silk, and ginger cock's hackle wrapped under the wings...this fly is about two inches in length.

Bowlker's second dressing is called the King's Fisher or the Peacock Fly:

This is also a salmon fly and is seen at the same time as the Dragon Fly. The wings are made from the feather from the neck or tail of the peacock, the body of deep green mohair, warped with light green silk, and a jay's feather striped blue and white wrapped under the wings.

Sometimes small beads were used to represent eyes on the great heads of Dragon Flies, a device which 20th century reservoir trout fishermen were to reinvent with great enthusiasm.

Bates is admirable on the subject and one cannot help quoting him again:

Why did the salmon prefer a simulated 'fly', a dragon fly, moth or butterfly? They didn't find them at sea, and their memory of them from the time when the salmon were parr or smolts would be remote.

On their return to their native rivers, while nature stifles their hunger, they do sample tidbits occasionally, however, and perhaps because of conditioned reflex, salmon instinctively react to the motion of small moving objects that might be a variety of prey. The correctly dressed salmon fly has a pulsating wing and hackles, which give a rhythmic action which incites strikes. This peculiarity of shape and motion seems to trigger this reflex.

All that remains is to make the fly visible to the fish in the correct size and colours for various conditions. The often quoted similarity of the classic salmon fly shape to that of butterflies or moths seems largely to be an inherited coincidence, but it was grasped by fly dressers because it could be developed into beautiful patterns inspired by the insects themselves.

(J. D. Bates, *The Art of the Atlantic Salmon Fly*, 1990)

Bowlker has at long last given us a reasonably effective salmon fishing outfit: a strong rod, a reel, a strong line made of either tough silk or twisted horsehair about 50 to 80 yards long and tapered to make casting easy.

He tells us that in most places the artificial fly is the only bait used for salmon 'being far superior to any other' - which is the first time that anybody said this - and he gives an interesting estimate of the principal English salmon rivers:

The Thames salmon are reckoned to exceed in quality those of any other river; but those in the rivers Severn and Wye are excellent in their kind and are first in season of any in England.

CHAPTER SIX

Points of Departure

It is interesting that many of the new developments and refinements in flyfishing and in fly design came not from the southern chalkstreams, as chalkstream fishermen like Waller Hills liked to imagine, but from the provinces, the Midlands, the limestone rivers of Derbyshire like the Dove, from Venables on the rivers of Ireland and Cheshire, and later from Stewart on the Borders. Somehow, in the early 1700s, a new mood seemed to be captured and to spread among fishermen in many parts of England, and for that matter in Scotland too, in which the fly became more important and more fascinating than bait.

It was a small movement of opinion, it is true, but it was noticeable for the first time: a new way of thinking that began to move flyfishing, imperceptibly, away from bait even in some cases when bait might have been a more effective method for taking fish. Such opinions had not been held before but they were beginning to be held now, admittedly by a small minority of fishers, influenced perhaps by a popular playwright and poet, John Gay. He was a Somerset man, born in Barnstable, but he achieved fame in London with works like *The Beggars Opera* which was said to have driven the Italian opera out of England for a whole season. His *Rural Sports* was a best seller. In it he described why he gave up bait for the fly:

Around the steel no tortur'd worm shall twine,
No blood of living insect stain my line,
Let me, less cruel, cast feathered hook
With pliant rod athwart the pebbled brook
Silent among the mazy margins stray
And with fur-wrought fly delude the prey.

Rural Sports, inscribed to Alexander Pope, was published in 1713. It was significant of a growing mood, no more than that, and a minority mood, for bait fishing was universally in favour as indeed it still is, but it was a sign of a change that was taking place among more thoughtful fishermen who felt uneasy about the indifference of many anglers to the pain they inflicted on the living creatures they used as bait:

Now of these water frogs, if you intend to fish with a frog for a pike, you are to chose the yellowist you can get, for that the pike ever likes best. And thus use your frog that he may continue long alive. Put your hook into his mouth, which you may easily do from the middle of April till August, and then the frog's mouth grows up, and he continues so for at least six months without eating, but is sustained none but He whose name is Wonderful knows how: I say, put your hook, I mean the arming-wire, through his mouth and out at his gills; and then with a fine needle and silk sew the upper part of his leg, with only one stitch, to the arming-wire of your hook; or tie the frog's leg, above the upper joint, to the arming -wire; and,in so doing, use him as though you loved him, that is harm as little as you may possibly, that he may live longer.

(Izaak Walton in *The Compleat Angler*)

Yet Walton was a kindly and considerate man and would have been surprised and probably hurt at anyone's sympathy for a frog which had clearly been created by the God of Nature for the benefit of fishermen and the satisfaction of pike.

48

Not that empathy for frogs or worms featured all that strongly in the growing preference for the fly. What was clearly more important was the skill and delicacy in casting a fly to a rising trout, the visible rise and take and the fascination of creating the illusion of life from fur and feather. It became, as indeed it still is, an intellectual stimulus, as well as satisfying the primitive instincts of the hunter.

This did not of course apply to those, and there were many, who fished for food. There are frequent contemporary accounts of fishermen taking baskets of twelve dozen trout, some for sale, some to be supplied by parish priests to the poor of a village. In most of these cases the worm would be essential. Even in the case of Venables, whom we have already quoted, although he preferred to fish the fly he was very much an all-round angler and most of his book was taken up with bait. We have to wait until 1810 for the publication of the first book that was to be devoted entirely to the fly.

This was George Scotcher's *Fly Fisher's Legacy* published at Chepstow, in South Wales a small town in those days which was unlikely to have had a publisher, a fact which has stimulated some curiosity about Mr Scotcher.

In 1974 the Honeydun Press published a facsimile edition together with an essay on Scotcher by Jack Heddon in which it is suggested that Scotcher was a pen name adopted by a local doctor, Mark Willet, who was in business as a chemist at 33 Moor Street, Chepstow, and may have owned a printing press as early as 1805.

Heddon, with John Simpson the antiquarian bookseller, were directors of the Honeydun Press and the reproduction of the Scotcher Book is of a remarkably high standard. Scotcher illustrated nineteen trout flies in colour - the first coloured illustration of flies - and gave the dressings of twenty-six. Heddon points out that Scotcher, Salter (*The Modern Angler,*

49

1802) the two Bowlkers and Robert Lascelles (*Angling*, 1811) all fished the fly upstream. Scotcher used only a point fly instead of a point and two droppers which had been the common practice until his time. Heddon goes on:

> There is sufficient evidence to convince any unbiased jury beyond any reasonable doubt that 18th Century flies were fished on the surface. Let me make it quite clear. This was not dry fly fishing as we know it.

This is of course true. There is a distinction between a floating fly and a dry fly. If we take the Berners or the Cotton patterns we can see that efforts were made to imitate the natural insect but little or no effort to imitate its behaviour and stance on the water. In contrast, the dry fly of the latter part of the 19th century, the flies of Hall and Marryat, were specifically designed to float on the water in a way that created the illusion of the float of the mayfly and the olive, that is to say with the wings cocked and the body of the fly upheld largely by the hackles. The difference is one of a more sophisticated design, not necessarily of intent. Hall and Marryat in the 1880s were simply making a better job of the floater than their ancestors.

However, we have been diverted and have left Scotcher for too long so we had better catch up. The main problem in his book is his difficulty in the naming of flies. Most of the natural flies of his time had many names from their regional and local origins, such as Ash Fly, Woodcock Fly, Cannon Fly, Downhill Fly, even an Apple Tree Fly, which all turned out to be the same insect, whatever that was, I have for the moment forgotten. So far as he was concerned he must have suffered a good deal of bewilderment and frustration trying to identify for example the winged brown, called variously Red Fly, Peacock Fly, Dark Brown, Dark Claret, etc - he added the etcetera to indicate that there must be some more names somewhere. On the flies he knew he was pretty good. He described the iron blue quite well:

> ...in shape as the Blue Dun but much smaller, the wings a clear purple, the body reddish dark purple, legs almost white and two whisks at the tail.

And his dressing was simple but effective: a dark blue dun hackle and a reddish purple silk for the body. He gave good advice, preferring a stiffer rod as it gave more control and greater accuracy in casting. He used a tapered horsehair line, a multiplying reel and only one fly on his cast.

His advice on fishing was sound. When a fish rises to take your fly, he said, you must be sure not to strike until he has taken it into his mouth, especially if it be a large fish. How many rises have we all missed by not taking that advice.

I think he must have known that his classification of flies was faulty but all he could do was to list the names of those he knew and relate them as far as possible to the natural. The worst was the alder which was known by eight other vernacular names, among them the curious title of Bastard Caddis.

He had a good word for the seatrout - sewin they are called in Wales - and advised that one should fish for them in the morning or in the evening with gaudy flies: a red cock hackle - from his description we would call it a furnace hackle - a black body of ostrich herl ribbed with silver with the hackle, ruffed down over it between the ribs. He warned about the power of a fresh-run sewin and told his readers to use 'good sound gut for your bottom.'

Where does Scotcher come in the pantheon of flyfishers? Pretty high, I think. He laid the basis of knowledge which would lead the way to Ronalds and through Ronalds to Halford who in due course spread the word about the dry fly to Theodore Gordon in America and from America to the rest

51

of the world.

Without the scientific knowledge of Ronalds, Scotcher tried to sort out the confusion of regional and local names for the natural insect and if he failed it was in many ways a glorious failure for it showed not only the absurdity of using numerous names for the same insect but the need for reducing the eight names of the alder to one and matching it to the corresponding scientific name so that there could be no doubt of its identity. Within a few years this very challenge was to be taken up by Alfred Ronalds.

In the meantime changes were taking place in many fly patterns, giving them new shapes, the creation not of copies but of illusions of insects, general patterns that were divorced from the standard floaters that we have seen from the *Treatyse* to the Bowlkers. One of the first changes to take place was to lower the wings of the fly. Instead of being upright they were lowered to point towards the rear of the hook, lying close to the body dressing, and the legs were also shaped to the rear to give a sleek shape to the whole artifical fly so that, when fished downstream, it made what was called 'a good entry' into the water.

These flies were fished a few inches below the surface, moving from across the stream into the main flow and curling round towards the angler's bank at possibly the deepest point that they reached, maybe six inches or a foot below the surface. In one or two fishing books of the 1700s there are first brief references to this way of fishing - the wet fly downstream. The wet flies were no longer in a true sense flies, but became suggestions of some kind of swimming water bug, possibly a small fish struggling against the current, being swept away after failing to make headway.

Another development retained the concept of a fly but one that had been tumbled and broken in the current, perhaps a fly that had failed to leave its nymphal shuck, or an imago, a spinner, that had laid its eggs on the water and was being tumbled downstream dead or dying just below the surface. It could also have been a fly that was just hatched and was making an effort to lift off from the surface.

These flies, which were mainly used in upstream wet fly fishing, were more or less straggling tufts of feathers on a hook with a slim body that suggested a drowned fly. The first account we have of them dates back to the late 1700s but of course they may well have been used long before that time. Typical upstream wet flies that we know of from that time are the Grouse Hackle, which consists of a slim yellow silk body with a hackle made from a small soft feather from a hen grouse; the Broughton's Point, invented about 1830 by a Penrith shoemaker; The Hofland's Fancy which came into use about the same time, and of course the Orange Partridge which must date back to the early 1700s if not before.

The man who was the great exponent of upstream wet fly fishing was an Edinburgh lawyer, W. C. Stewart, whose book *The Practical Angler* was first published in 1857 and republished many times since, the last in 1919. Although it was written in the mid- nineteenth century he refers to a method that was used to fish the Teviot streams of the Scottish Borders by a great angler, James Baillie, in the late 1700s.

I have a great affection for Stewart. He was emphatic about the need to fish the fly upstream:

> The great error of fly fishing as usually practised...is that the angler fishes downstream whereas he should fish up.

He gave his reasons. The angler by approaching the fish from behind was less visible; the hook was pulled into the mouth of the trout and not away from it; there was less disturbance to the water; and the flies had a more natural appearance as they

53

drifted down with the stream rather than being pulled across it. He echoed what we say nowadays when we talk about presentation, and he did it with courtesy and kindness (apart from a mild swipe at Francis Francis of *The Field* magazine who he thought had been critical of the way the Scots fished their flies), either on top or a few inches below the surface of the water. Stewart took pains to explain:

> The moment the flies alight - being the only one in which the trout take the artificial fly for a live one - is the most deadly in the whole cast [but] there is no reason for keeping them on the surface, they will be quite as attractive a few inches under water.

He was a nice man, Stewart: I wish I'd known him and I thought of him quite a lot as I fished some of his Border rivers, using a more modern rod and line but with the same flies, though only a point fly instead of the three, possibly four, he would have used. He was very particular about his flies, and generous minded too, for he did not take credit for their design, giving that to a much older man, James Baillie, for whom we have no dates but he must have fished the Borders during the time of the French Revolution or at the latest the Napoleonic wars.

Stewart's patterns were very thinly dressed compared with those of the tackle shops which he said were far too bushy. Stewart, who was not an entomologist, called them spiders, which 'resembled the natural insect in shape...in its extreme lightness and neatness of form.'

He did not say what natural insect he had in mind but he gave the impression that it did not matter all that much. The rivers he fished were fast flowing, the duns did not ride the waters as they do on the chalkstreams, the flies passed the trout at speed either on top of the water or just under the surface and if his patterns gave the illusion of a natural fly then that was all that mattered. Here they are, the famous three:

Black spider: A small hook covered in brown silk and the head hackle being the small feather of the cock starling.

Red spider: A yellow silk body and the hackle from a small feather from the outside wing of the landrail.

Dun spider: A body of dun silk and hackle the ash-coloured feather from the outside wing of the dotterel or from inside wing of the starling.

He also used winged flies of a simple design, some of them for loch fishing, such as Woodcock and Orange, Teal and Green, Grouse and Yellow and various mallard-winged flies such as we use today.

He was not a conservationist in the modern sense. In the Border rivers there were plenty of fish, an unlimited supply, or what seemed to be unlimited, to take home for himself and his friends. No doubt some good trout passed round the lawyer's chambers on the Monday mornings. He quotes James Baillie as killing an average of 12-14 lbs of trout in only four or five hours fishing and he said you could do more or less the same if you took the advice that he gave to fish upstream.

Stewart's tackle was a great help in allowing him to cast against the wind. He wore waterproof stockings, had a fairly stiff spliced rod 10 or 12 foot long with a bamboo top and a hickory butt, a plain brass reel with a mixed horsehair and silk 'winch line', as he called it. Later he went over to pure silk lines which he must have greased and dried after every expedition. His cast was of triple gut with a point of 'picked' gut tapering to the flies. His hooks were round bend and he used the water knot to join line to gut.

He was a great enthusiast. Angling, he said, becomes a

passion and he insisted that flyfishing was the cleanest, the most elegant and gentlemanly of all the methods of capturing trout. He waded upstream, casting to the rise or, if there were no rises, to the food stream, casting frequently, letting the flies drift only a yard or so, then casting again, a little further, to one side, to another side, moving upstream reasonably fast, covering a great deal of water. Cast as frequently as possible, he says, and I would suspect that half the time the flies were on the surface of the water and the other half just a few inches below.

He went at times to Loch Leven and though he preferred to fish the fly there, if he could, often the best way was trolling a minnow or a parr tail bait, or using the worm on what we still call Stewart tackle, but he was not all that keen on bait fishing and he used the loch flies whenever he could.

I have no account of him fishing for salmon, though he fished the Tweed many times for the trout, but he records in one of the last editions of his book that in 1866 a salmon fisherman on the River Awe, William Muir of Innistrynich, caught a well-conditioned brown trout of 39.5 lbs which was 3 foot 9 inches long with a girth of 2 foot 2.25 inches. It was taken on a small salmon fly and played for two hours before being landed.

Having read Stewart's book a number of times. I have felt drawn close to him and to his friend James Baillie. This does not occur with many other books but there is something about the way Steward wrote which speaks directly to my own feelings. He was a great man and I wish I had known him. He lived to a ripe old age, as many fishermen do, and always, as he said, he had a feeling of thankfulness for the past, and bright hopes for the future, for the coming of another spring and another season.

CHAPTER SEVEN

The Arrival of Ronalds

B y the time Scotcher was writing in South Wales and Baillie was fishing the Borders anglers were already able to fish their flies upstream or down, on the surface, or just below. But fishing upstream was slow to develop. Primitive tackle hindered its success. Certain conditions were needed and the wind was often decisive. John Worlidge set out the advantages of fishing the fly upstream as long ago as 1698:

> In a swift stream where the bottom is hard and not too deep if you go into the middle of it and cast your Fly up against the Stream, the Trout that lies upon the Fin in such strong Currents, and discerns you not, being behind him, presently takes your bait.

The tapered and greased silk line was efficient in giving greater accuracy against the wind but was far less buoyant than horsehair, nor was it so good for dibbling the fly downstream. The new silkworm gut was admirable in many ways but again horsehair points had the advantage of buoyancy. This led to short casting with a long rod, the technique used by William Shipley on the Dove in 1838:

> Let your flies float gently down the water, working them gradually towards you, and making a fresh cast every two or

three yards you fish. We distinctly recommend frequent casting. A fish generally takes the fly immediately it has touched the water - providing it has been delicately and lightly flung - and the quick repetition of casting whisks the water out of your flies and line, and consequently keeps them drier and lighter than if they were left to float a longer time in the water.

Whisking the water out of your flies and line is more or less equivalent to false casting to dry the fly and so allow it to float better, though 'false casting' was not a phrase that was in use at that time. We are sometimes inclined to be confused by words and the meaning of words. There is no difference between whisking the water out of your fly and false casting to do so except in the words we give to them, and words come into and go out of fashion.

In my own case, when I was experimenting with a horsehair line, it was quite natural to whisk the surplus water out of the fly when casting upstream and when I did so the fly would float for a short while before sinking into the surface film, becoming what we would now call an emerger pattern. Sometimes it would sink below the surface which would mean that in a matter of a drift of several feet, it would behave first as a dry fly, then an emerger, and then a wet fly.

The great achievement of the 1880s, which we will come to in another chapter, was of course to design our flies in such a way that without floatants they would float for a much longer time on the surface of the water than had been possible before. They would indeed sink, often before the end of a drift, but even when they did so they could be dried again by false casting or whisking.

Before the full potential of the floating fly could be developed new ideas had to come and further inventions had to be made. Dressings for flies were needed that would lift them up as much as possible away from clinging particles of water, new rods and lines were needed that would cast the flies more easily and lightly and a greater distance than before, and there had to be a greater knowledge of the natural insect. All these things were to arrive in the remarkable 19th century, from about 1800 to 1880.

Scotcher took us some way towards defining the natural fly and its corresponding artificial but more was wanted. This was realised by a Staffordshire man, Alfred Ronalds, who for many years carried out experiments on his local river, the Blythe near Uttoxeter.

He was a fine flyfisherman and he was also a brilliant watercolour artist and he set out to paint the natural fly and the artificial, side by side, which were reproduced in full colour together with the appropiate dressings in his book *The Fly-Fisher's Entomology* published in 1836.

This was a great step forward. For the first time fishermen could see the natural fly with its scientific name and compare it with the artificial and on the next page read the way the artificials were tied.

Ronalds' flies were wet flies, a point fly and two droppers, designed to be fished upstream or down, whatever was the easiest or most appropriate to conditions. He suggested using a tapered horsehair line as being the easiest to cast.

Ronalds was modest. He says his book must be treated as 'the amusement of an amateur' based on his own personal experience. He starts with a description of the trout, and later the grayling, He describes where they are to be found, how to see the food stream, tells us that the fish are alarmed by vibrations but not by conversation or even gunshots, and from feeding them dead houseflies covered in cayenne pepper and mustard concluded that if trout had a sense of taste it was not particularly sensitive.

He was good at describing how to fish:

59

When a fish has just risen at a natural object it is well for the fisherman to try to throw into the curl occasioned by the rise and left as a mark for him, but should the undulations have nearly died away, before he can throw to the spot, then he should throw as nearly as he can judge a yard or two above it and allow the flies to float down to the supposed place of the fish; if a rise does not occur it may be concluded that the fish has removed without seeing the flies; he may then try a yard or two on each side of the place where the curl appeared, when he may probably have a rise and may possibly hook the fish providing he has the knack of striking, which knack like all other is only acquired by practice.

It is not quite clear whether he was talking of the olives, the upwinged flies, or the caddis, in his advice to give movement to the fly:

When the fly is thrown on the stream some little resemblance of life must be given to it; this I imagine may best be accomplished by throwing across and down the current...the current will then act against part of the line lying on the water and cause the fly to sail over the same side [as the angler] yet still to float down a little as the natural fly when struggling might be supposed to do.

That must be the clearest description we have had so far of the way to fish a wet fly downstream. On the subject of wading he suggests waterproof fishing boots 'as used in Scotland' or what he describes as 'India-rubber overalls, as about Sheffield' - a peculiar phrase which suggests some kind of breast wader, or is that going too far?

He describes and gives an illustration of the refraction of light as it enters the water with the consequent advice to fishermen to avoid being seen by the fish. He seems to have fished the Dove as well as the Blythe and advises that:

in brooks, where fish are looking upstream for the flies and other food which float down to them, good sport is be had in bright weather by walking up the middle, and casting either fly or worm before you, especially where the water is broken, either by running over stones, or by tumbling over ledges of rocks, etc. into little pools or basins. And observe, that fish cannot see behind them; all optics forbid it, especially when they are not looking out sharply.

That passage includes a description of what American flyfishers now call fishing 'pocket water', a most useful method.

Trout, in his experience on the Blythe, made a strict inspection of the food coming down to them; sometimes they take something in their mouths, sometimes avidly, sometimes more slowly, and frequently eject it instantly as being unfit to eat:

> This seems to favour the notion that if a Trout has not a taste similar to our own, he may be endowed with some equivalent species of sensation. It may also account for his taking of a *nondescript artificial* fly [his italics]; but it furnishes no plea to quacks and bunglers, who, inventing or espousing a new theory, whereby to hide their want of skill or spare their pains, would kill all fish with one fly, as some doctors would cure all diseases by one pill. If a Trout rejects the brown hive bee at the time he greedily swallows the March-brown fly, it is clear that the imitation should be as exact as possible of the last, and as dissimilar as possible to the first.

He anticipates Skues' method of emptying the stomach contents of a trout into a baby's plate, though Ronalds used a large cup of water, and he clearly carries out an autopsy rather than emptying the stomach with a marrow spoon:

61

A convenient method of examining the contents of the stomach is to put the materials into a hair seive and pump clean water upon them; when parted and sufficiently clean the whole contents may be put into a large cup of clean water, for examination. This method of testing the actual food of the fish in different waters and seasons will give the angler most valuable information respecting his game. Worms are the earliest bait that can be employed with success after the winter; then comes the troller's turn, with his spinning minnow or bleak for the larger Thames trout; and the fly fisher will find the fish in the humour for feeding on the various insects that skim the surface of the brook, as the advancing spring brings forth its teeming myriads, and peoples the glad waters with winged life and animation.

His flies could be bought from Mr Eaton at 67 Crooked Lane in the City of London and he advises that the flies for grayling need a more delicate hand and a quicker eye than for trout, and he recommends the use of smaller flies upon the finest gut. He gives some advice on how to cast a fly which is good as far as it goes but concludes:

An attempt to describe all the precautions and manipulations requisite for throwing a fly successfully and gracefully would be as hopeless a task as that of trying to teach dancing by words.

The more one reads Ronalds, and I suppose by now I have read him several times, the more one gets the impression that he was a man of great balance and common sense, intensely curious about the behaviour of fish and insects and never satisfied by the opinions current about them at the time.

He comes very close after a while, almost as though he is thinking along the same lines that we do today. He and Stewart have a particular quality.

There is one thing to warn you about Ronalds: his scientific classification of flies is out of date. For the blue dun - he still uses that name for the large dark olive - he says it belongs to the genus Potamanthus and its species is rufescens. For us it is Baetis rhodani. For the iron blue he says that it is a diptera of the genus Cloeon whereas to us it is either Baetis pumilous or, the other kind, Baetis niger. That can't be helped. It does not in the slightest detract from the value of his book to his own and to succeeding generations. For the first time we are able to see the natural fly and its corresponding artificial, side by side, in full colour, though Ronalds' artificials are much more wet flies than dry (see p.155)

CHAPTER EIGHT

Butterflies for Salmon

Little has been heard about salmon for some time, not since Franck and Barker in the 17th century and Bowlker in the 18th, and it is noticeable that it is English visitors rather than the locals who wanted to write about fishing the great salmon rivers of Scotland and Ireland.

In both those countries salmon fishing rights were Crown property nominally held by the barons and the great lairds. For trout the right to fish came from the ownership of land either on one or both banks of the river.

Salmon fishing in Scotland was fairly easily obtained - as Franck found - and not only for visitors. Robert the Bruce (1274-1329), King of Scotland, a descendant of one of the Norman barons, De Bruis, was a lord of Annandale and gave its inhabitants a free hand over the fishings. So far as Franck's journey was concerned the factor of the Queensberry estate at Drumlanrig in Dumfriesshire, Peter Kennedy, says:

> In all probability, fishing rights were not considered to be valuable in those days and not exercised in full, so owners allowed anyone to fish. After all there were probably not many travellers like Richard Franck. In the past, salmon were not regarded as anything but very ordinary food.

There is a suggestion by E. J. Malone that it was the influence of English officers who brought flyfishing to Ireland during the occupation. It could be so. Robert Venables was commander-in-chief in Ulster under Cromwell and took his fishing rods with him on his campaign, as did General Bedell Smith in Europe during the Second World War.

Ireland has legendary stories about the salmon from the time of the Irish kings such as this recounted by Leslie Bryan of Trinity College library in Dublin:

> It is in the medieval tale *The Pursuit of Diarmaid and Grainne* from the Finn or Ossianic Cycle. It concerns two eloping lovers who during their adventures escaping from her older husband, Finn mac Cumaill, meet a young warrior named Mudan. He fastens a straight long rod from a quicken tree (mountain ash or rowan tree). He attaches a hair and hook to the rod and puts a holly berry on the hook. He catches three fish by this method.

There are constant references to salmon in the Finn Cycle. The salmon eat nuts and are then caught. They who catch the salmon obtain 'impas' meaning wisdom.

It was the Irish, round about 1800-1820, who were responsible for a small revolution in salmon flies which had a great influence on the Scots. Before then, the flies, taking their shape from large trout flies, based partly on dragonflies, were rather drab affairs for some reason or other best known to their makers.

The Irish suddenly introduced vivid and exotic feathers and bodies for fishing the Erne and the Shannon. They called them 'butterflies'. Bates tells the story how Pat McKay visited the millinery shop at Ballyshannon near the Erne in north-west Ireland:

> He must have been amazed at what he found in that Irish shop: silk threads and flosses of every colour; skins of the golden pheasant, the cock-of-the-rock, blue chatterer, Indian crow,

parrot, macaw, and other exotic feathers from South America and other far-flung parts of the world. This was the heyday of British world trade and unusual imports were common. While Ballyshannon was not a noted seaport, the profusion of salmon in the river Erne made it a mecca for anglers and therefore a center of fly dressers. The noted Rogan family lived near the bridge at Ballyshannon. Competition among fly dressers was intense.

The news of the new flies was brought to London by an enterprising fly dresser, William Blacker, from Dublin, who opened a shop at 54 Dean Street, Soho, around 1820 and from there the flies reached the Scots. One of McKay's first patterns was the Golden Butterfly. Here it is:

Tag: Fine silver twist and gold floss silk
Tail: A golden pheasant topping and barred wood duck
Butt: Black ostrich herl
Body: Yellow floss silk
Ribbing: Medium gold twist
Throat: Three toppings curled downwards
Wing: A topping applied edgeways on each side of the body to curve inward, both ends meeting midway along the tail; also one large topping tied on top to curve upwards.
Cheeks: A cock-of-the-rock feather on each side tied high and edgewise, and a kingfisher feather on each side tied low.
Head: Black ostrich herl and black tapered thread, varnished.

McKay, Rogan and Blacker were artists. The creation of a salmon fly became an art, a jewel upon a hook, a lure for the fisherman as much as for the fish and both were taken with it. The Butterflies, the Golden Parson, and all the beautiful and complex designs that were to follow were the work of craftsmen intent upon producing the most lovely and delicate objects from fur and feather for the same creative reasons that Fabergé was to shape his complexities of jewels and William Morris his elaboration of textiles.

On some stretches of the Tweed the new exotic flies were banned. Tom Stoddart was against them but in due course the sheer pleasure of looking at them overcame a natural dislike of the invader. They also caught fish. Within another 50 years a considerable effort was made to explain why this should be so.

That great Victorian George M. Kelson was an inventor of various kinds of fishing tackle, most of which were patented. They included the Kelson salmon rod, the Kelson gaff, the Kelson salmon line, the Kelson patent lever winch, the Kelson fishing coat and even a gadget to enable a one-armed angler to fish with a double-handed salmon rod, the butt of which was supported by a kind of sling round the fisherman's neck. Kelson said more than once that salmon fishing was a science and that like everything else in the universe it was governed by laws which he was able to interpret.

In 1895 he published privately a 500-page book, *The Salmon Fly*, which was more thorough and comprehensive than anything previously attempted. It contained many coloured paintings of salmon flies and some 200 detailed salmon fly dressings, many of them his own, with instructions how they should be used, such as:

> Supposing the bed of the river to be of a slatey nature...and the day dull, dark blue, dark claret, or even dark orange with black seal's fur or silk at the throat will form the body material. And where the fish will stand it a few or more strands of peacock herl should be added to any built wing. Spey fish object to herl: Usk fish adore it.

He never explained how he knew that salmon in some rivers objected to peacock herl and in other rivers did not. He went on

The supremely confident George M. Kelson

to say it was notorious that in several rivers the fish had been educated persistently to snub old patterns in favour of the new. These new patterns were the ones he had designed. And therefore, he argued, was it not indeed an achievement to present to the fish one of these new flies which the fish preferred to the others and which were so strongly attractive as to establish more or less permanently 'a decided taste in the fish so that he refuses other flies to wait for yours'. He put those last four words in italics - he was fond of italics - without explaining why or how the salmon knew that having refused an old pattern an irresistible new Kelson fly would be coming to him next. Kelson was a very odd character.

Some of the best fly patterns - one was the Blue Charm - had, so he believed, entirely lost their value

by passing through phases of irresponsible treatment and might well receive their congé from some reliable judicative source.

Unless there was some other meaning intended, which is doubtful, the reliable judicative source would have been Kelson himself. He was so self-confident about his judgment, for he had wide experience of many rivers, that he found it difficult to moderate his conceit. His claim of a supreme knowledge based on powers of observation given to few formed the basis of 'a methodical, organised and precise system of fishing' that was always ready to hand.

His 'special standard dressings' of flies covered every eventuality, every type of river and he even had a dressing, called Elsie (see p.164) for streams of uneven rocks temporarily or permanently located on the river bed.

Among his two hundred fly patterns he gave a dressing of the Golden Butterfly but attributed its invention to Traherne. It bore little relationship to the original dressed by Pat McKay some eighty years earlier. However, he did try hard to give credit to others, though perhaps not many. He gave unrestricted admiration to the creator of the Jock Scott salmon fly (see p.165). Nevertheless he was strongly attacked by the editor of *The Fishing Gazette*, R. B. Marston, for claiming fly patterns as his own or his father's when they had been tied by others.

He was never able to put forward a reasonable argument in

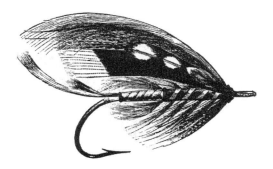

The Jock Scott - most famous of the Victorian salmon flies

favour of his 'scientific' approach to salmon fishing without abusing others who were either hostile to his views or might be hostile. For example, at the end of this perfectly sensible argument in favour of accurate observation and experiment:

> We have to make our own science before we can apply it. The facts we must build on are the habits and tastes of the salmon as affected by the variety of his natural surroundings, the predisposition he evinces for certain shades of colour and certain kinds of flies, the variations of water and weather and above all the mischief brought about by the preceding efforts of Fishermen destitute of all practical knowledge.

What he meant by 'mischief' is not clear; presumably salmon were disturbed in some way by those who had fished a beat before him, or so he imagined, but he does not explain how they were disturbed. One cannot help feeling that the more one tries to understand Kelson's meanings the more obscure they become. His egotism is so great, his dogmatism so widespread, his belief in himself and his theories so unchallengeable, that all must be accepted without question. That is the only explanation. It leads him to this kind of incoherence:

> It is happy for us latter-day Anglers that the 'specials' [the Kelson special fly patterns which he designed] came into existence and that they still live and that they afford so many proofs of their own masterful vitality in those very times when all other flies fail.

It is of course complete nonsense to say all other flies failed. The fully-dressed feathered flies that survived into the next century were modified dressings of flies which Kelson did not design - the Dunkeld, Hairy Mary, Garry Dog, Blue Charm and one or two others. Those he did design - the Variegated Sun Fly and others - did not survive more than a few years. It is rather sad. However, during his lifetime he had many disciples and was looked upon as an authority.

Kelson lost no chance in exercising that authority even in such matters as the right clothes for women to wear when salmon fishing. An article in a newspaper the *Daily Telegraph*, said that the Princess of Wales and her daughters fished in gowns made with skirts down to the ankle. Kelson's advice to Her Royal Highness was:

> [You] need a short skirt of tweed bound deeply round the hem with porpoise hide and worn over knickerbockers. This is made so it be buttoned right up, forming a sort of fishwife skirt and furnished with a big pocket for fly book and tackle.

If it is necessary to wade so as to cast over a favourite hole, waterproof overall fishing boots can be put on; but, as a rule, this is not found needful and few ladies use them. A high-legged pair of porpoise hide boots and thick woollen stockings are usually deemed sufficient as, if a fisherwoman must get wet, she will soon walk herself dry again.

Altogether it was a curious episode in flyfishing history in which a plume turned into a dragon fly and the dragon fly into a butterfly and intelligent men - for Kelson was certainly intelligent - tried to make sense of it all and failed. The sequel is in Chapter 18.

CHAPTER NINE

Springs and Origins

During Queen Victoria's reign (1837-1901) flyfishing developed with extraordinary speed. For hundreds of years men had fished in more or less the same way with what was essentially the same kind of tackle, the fixed line had given way to the running line, the reel and the landing net had arrived, but that was about all. But now, in Victorian times, a young man who started to fish in the 1840s and 50s would be using quite different rods, lines and flies - especially flies - by the time he was middle-aged. It was a revolutionary change.

Many influences - social, economic, technical development and research - contributed. This was the time of the great industrial development of Britain as the centre of a worldwide empire. Enormous changes were taking place. There were great movements of populations. By 1851 half the inhabitants of England were living in towns, 'a situation that had probably not existed before in a great country at any time in the world's history' (Trevelyan). The results were far-reaching.

An interpretation of the changed outlook among fishermen was given by a Scottish flyfisher, H. B. McCaskie, who was born towards the end of the Victorian era:

The railways...brought great new populations to the towns, among them many whose hearts were by a river while their bodies were pent in bricks and mortar. Before that time a man

75

fished because he lived beside a river and wanted something to fill in the gap between one hunting or shooting season and the next. He would stroll to the bank for the evening rise, or for the brisk hour or two in the middle of a spring day; a hardy northern angler might make a day of it but a fishing holiday was a thing unknown. The nearest approach we have to it is Col. Thornton's Sporting Tour in the Highlands undertaken in 1802 in the spirit of an explorer on safari.

For the reluctant town-dweller fishing ceased to be just a means of filling an unoccupied hour and became something symbolic and almost sacred, for it represented an escape from the dull world of reality. It was not long before this new feeling crept,

Richard Routledge models some early chest waders

76

either consciously or unconsciously, into our angling books. The works of Viscount Grey of Fallodon, H. T. Sher-ingham, William Caine and others owe their abiding charm to the joyous sense of escape that runs through them. Escape is a poor word, with something of the Freudian jargon clinging to it; the Greeks had a noble name for it and called it ecstasy: a standing aside: a withdrawal from the common world.

Viscount Grey of Fallodon (1862-1933) was British Foreign Secretary from 1905 to 1916. Before reaching Cabinet rank he wrote an admirable book of great charm on fly fishing which has been republished many times since. In it he describes the mood of the Londoner who wanted to go fishing:

If our work will let us escape on Friday evening, it is luxury; but even if we belong only to those in the middle state of happiness who will work till midnight or later on Friday, and can have the whole of Saturday and Sunday in the country we may still be splendidly well off, providing that we are careful to miss nothing. The earliest trains leave Waterloo, the usual place of departure for the Itchen or the Test, either at, or just before, six o'clock in the morning.

To leave London it is possible once a week even after late hours to get up in time for these early trains, and if you have no luggage (and you need have none if you go to the same place week after week) you will not find it difficult to get to the station. There are places where hansoms can be found even at these hours of the morning; they are not numerous, and they seem quite different from the hansoms that are abroad at more lively hours, but they can be found if you look for them in certain places.

The best plan however is to live within a walk of Waterloo, and as you cross the river in the early summer morning, you may feel more reconciled to London than at any other time, and understand Wordsworth's tribute to the sight from Westminster Bridge. I pass over the scene at Waterloo station, which at this hour is very different from the usual one, and the journey, on which perhaps one sleeps a little, though I have found that, while it is very easy to sleep sitting up in the later hours of the evening, it is necessary to lie down, if one wishes to sleep in the early hours of the morning.

At some time between eight and nine o'clock you step out of the train, and are in a few minutes among all the long desired things. Every sense is alert and every scent and everything seen or heard is noted with delight. You are grateful for the grass on which you walk, even for the soft country dust about your feet.

Small boys, for no particular reason at all, become suddenly fascinated by fishing. It comes upon them at a very early age, vivid, alive, fascinating, the source of dreams. T. C. Kingsmill Moore, in later life a judge of the Irish Supreme Court, was infected as an eight-year-old, and fishing literature simply burst on him when he went to Marlborough:

In the school library were all the standard works of the day, the Badminton volumes, Stewart's *Practical Angler* (still after a hundred years the best book for a boy) the earlier volumes of Halford, that high priest of chalkstream eclecticism, and most delightful of all angling books, Sir Edward Grey's *FlyFishing*.

Not four hundred yards from where I sat reading, the Kennet glided under White Horse hill, and from Preshute and Duck Bridges trout were on view. This land of chalkstream and meadows was strange country to me, and though boys were not allowed to fish, no one could bandage my eyes. Up and down stream I wandered. It was the hey-day of the water meadows, when carriers were kept clean and sluices in repair. Nowhere is life more teeming than in a water meadow when June is high, the air heavy with the scent of elder, water mint and sweet cicely, sedges and withy beds quivering with warblers and buntings, back waters a continual bustle of coot, dabchick and water hen. I lay on my face and saw the bright beetles and all the scurrying insects of the grass roots crawl under me, stood waist deep in the water to dip out the hiding nymphs, watched them turn into duns and then, shedding their last film, into the crystal of the spinner. The wild duck led her string of ducklings down stream and never noticed me, the trout sucked in a dun or

Viscount Grey of Falloden in 1915

swirled more energetically after an escaping sedge within a few yards of where I sat motionless. It was a lesson in 'Study to be quiet.'

(*A Man May Fish*, T. C. Kingsmill Moore, 1960)

Professors of English can be infected with the same feelings as small boys at Marlborough:

Fishing makes rivers my corrective lens; I see differently. Not only does the bird taking the mayfly signify a hatch, not only does the flash of color at the break of the riffle signify a fish feeding, but my powers uncoil inside me and I must determine which insect is hatching and what feeding pattern the trout has established. Then I must properly equip myself and properly approach the fish and properly present my imitation. I am engaged in a hunt that is more than a hunt, for the objects of the hunt are mostly to be found within myself, in the nature of my response and action. I am on a Parsifalian quest. I must be scientist, technician, athlete, perhaps even a queer sort of poet.

(*Bright Rivers*, Nick Lyons, 1977)

It is difficult to know what to call this new mood, this Parsifalian quest, if that is what it is, for whatever description is chosen - introspection, autobiographical, a search into one's self, the use of fishing to make a commentary on life - it does not explain why it has not happened before, why people have been writing like this only in the last fifty or a hundred years. It cannot be purely a preoccupation of intellectuals for there were plenty of intellectuals before Grey, men like Humphrey Davy for example, president of the Royal Society (1778 -1829) but they merely wrote on practical matters. There was nothing like a flyfishing philosophy at all before the 1890s, not a metaphysician in sight. Then, suddenly, Grey, Moore, Lyons and so many others, one after another, analysing their feelings, trying to explain their relationship to the rivers and fish. The broadcaster and writer Howard Marshall sums it all up:

> Fishing is an integration with the springs and origins of human existence It takes us back into pre-history to shake hands with the cave man.
>
> *(Reflections on a River*, 1967)

Certainly, within quite a short time, as time goes, flyfishermen have become essayists, nature writers, philosophers, probing into themselves and their surroundings, studying the abrupt changes that affect them when they leave the cabinet room, the lecture hall, the pressures of the city, to take part in a primitive hunt in the wilderness, which is more than a hunt, a relationship of the present to the past, a correlation of experience. It is of interest and significance that the four writers that we have quoted and no doubt many others that we have not quoted but who have been saying much the same things are, or were dry fly fishermen.

CHAPTER TEN

The Dry Fly

A s Professor Joad used to say: it all depends what you *mean* by a dry fly. To Halford and his followers in the 1880s it meant a split-wing floater. To David Foster of Ashbourne in the mid-1800s it meant a well-hackled fly that floated longer than a badly-hackled fly. To George Pulman of Axminster also in the mid-1800s it meant a fly that he had just taken out of his box to replace a fly that had become soaked.

The two major innovators of the new style of flydressing which gave the fly a longer float were James Ogden of Cheltenham, and David Foster of Ashbourne. Both were guides and tackle dealers, Ogden on the Gloucestershire Coln and Foster on the Derbyshire Dove. Of these two Foster has the greater scope.

He was born at Burton-on-Trent in 1815, worked for Allcocks of Redditch, tackle manufacturers, started his own tackle business at Ashbourne in 1841 and died, so far as we know, some time in the late 1870s, or perhaps a little later. He left numerous manuscript records of bait and fly fishing which his sons published posthumously in 1882 as *The Scientific Angler*.

Foster gives the first detailed and comprehensive description of how to fish the dry fly, and he may have taken the word 'dry fly' from Pulman in preference to the then more commonly-used term, the 'floating fly'. He recommends the dry fly above all other methods:

> The dry fly system is...by far the most scientific and artistic way of alluring trout or grayling and well-fished streams will yield more and heavier dishes of fish to it than any other method or system of angling whatever.

He makes his flies in the new way which was later widely adopted. After the body is tied, fibres from a bird's wing feather are tied doubled to make upright wings, and after the wings are tied the hackle for the legs should be tied 'ample and full' to assist floatation. This was the first time that this important change in flydressing had been described.

It was particularly important on fast streams that the flies must be cast 'a few feet above the indication of a rise and then allowed to float over [the fish]'. On slower streams he did not mind whether the fly was cast up or down or across as long as it got a good float:

> With the duns the wings must be full and erect, or 'cock-up' as it is sometimes designated, so as to admit the fly to be comparatively dry for some little time when, becoming saturated, a few backwards and forwards whisks of the line and rod should be given before the delivery of the cast again. This is repeated whenever the flies become saturated as by so doing the trouble of repeatedly changing the lure is greatly lessened.

There, for the first time, is the full description of the dry fly technique even down to the details of making a bush of hackle to give a longer float. Moreover Foster was well aware that the artificial fly must be regarded from below, where the trout would see it, rather than looking down on it when the fly was being designed and tied. In this he was well in advance of Halford (see p.93).

Foster sorted out his flies by what he called 'the shade' of the dressing. His big mayfly pattern anticipated those of the chalkstreams. The body was made from wheaten straw, the wings dyed mallard, Canadian wood duck or Egyptian goose,

David Foster: first to describe the 'dry fly system'

the body ribbed with red-brown silk, and for the whisks three strands of a partridge tail feather (see also Appendix, p.168)

We cannot, unfortunately, give the date when Foster wrote his description of dry fly fishing. It would be after 1840 and probably sometime before the end of the 1860s, approximately twenty or thirty years before the first split-wing floaters designed by H. S. Hall were seen on the chalkstreams.

Just after Foster died came a revolutionary change in rods and lines which enabled the fly to be cast not only against a strong wind but for a greater distance and with greater accuracy. First came the six-sided split cane rod.

The English had been the first to realise the value of the use of the outer skin of bamboo in fly rods because of its strength and flexibility but it was the Americans, notably Hiram Leonard, who were to develop the six-sided cane rods. Leonard invented new milling machines for the cane and made ferrules at great speed from the correct size of tubing. His mass production method 'developed a labor-intensive craft into a lucrative industry' (Paul Schullery, *American Fly Fishing* 1989).

The English chalkstream fishermen were curiously reluctant to accept these new rods to begin with. They dismissed them 'as a transient American fad'(*Baily's Magazine*, 1899). They were soon proved wrong. A London lawyer, G. E. M. Skues, said his Leonard was 'the world's best rod' and lavished praise on it in many magazine articles.

American skill and inventiveness also provided the new braided, oiled silk lines, heavy lines to match the power of the new cane rods so that they could be cast better. Fishermen were at last released from much of the tyranny of the wind. Then came the new flies, the split-winged floaters. Skues summed up the change:

> The things which made the dry fly generally possible were the coming of the heavy American braided oiled silk line and the split cane rod. I remember buying my first length of oiled silk line in 1877 but I knew so little of its purpose that I used it for sea fishing and it was I think in the eighties that, stimulated by American progress in the building of split canes, our makers

began to build split canes suitable for carrying those heavy lines. The heavy line was needed to deliver the fly dry and to put it into the wind; the split cane or wood rod on the same lines

Henry Sinclair Hall: creator of the split-wing floater

was necessary to deliver the heavy line. With the hour came the men. Mr H. S. Hall, Mr G. S. Marryat and Mr F. M. Halford who evolved from the poor feeble types of dry flies of the seventies the efficient dry fly of the eighties and the present day.

The man who first tied the split-wing floaters was Henry Sinclair Hall (1848-1934). We have this information from Skues (see page 172) though it was only publicised at the time in *The Field* magazine. Hall was a schoolmaster at Clifton College, head of the military side of the school, and joint author of textbooks on algebra and geometry. His passion was fishing and he invented the modern eyed hook which replaced the snelled hooks - hooks with no eyes that were whipped directly on to gut.

Hall, Marryat and Skues fished the Abbots Barton water of the Itchen above Winchester, met frequently and exchanged many ideas. It was a most inventive time. Marryat must share a part of the credit for he wrote frequently to Hall during term time with many ideas about flydressing.

The secret of Hall's new flies were their lightness and the way he used slips of feather from two opposing wings that gave a nice balance to the body. The wings were able to balance the fall of the fly so that it fell cocked on the water with the wings upright, a better method than the folded wing fibres of Foster's dressings. Like Foster, however, he recommended a goodly bunch of stiff hackle tied in after the wings had been secured. The fly on the water was balanced on the hackle points and the tail whisks. The bodies were made of quill rather than absorbent materials for in those days there were no floatants and the flies had to be dried by false casting

Neither Hall nor Marryat courted publicity but they showed the new flies to commercial flydressers at Winchester - Mrs Cox and John Hammond - as well as Holland of Salisbury, and very soon the news spread and they were on the market.

The market would have been ready and anxious to have them, for publicity about 'fishing the dry fly' was in *The Field* as early as 1857 in an article by the angling editor Francis

Francis who wrote:

> I recommend the angler to try a dry fly - e.g. suppose the angler
> sees a rising fish, let him allow his casting line and fly to dry for
> a minute previous to making a cast and then throw over the fish
> and let it float down without motion. This is a killing plan when
> fishing with duns.

These were, of course. at that time, the traditional Ronald-type
flies which, as Skues pointed out, mostly fell on their sides and
did not float with their wings cocked. Not that it mattered a
great deal. The new idea of a dry fly was what mattered. It
conjured up the idea of a fairy-like creature, light as air,
floating beautifully on top of the water and irresistible to the
fish.

Yet the origin of the phrase 'dry fly' had nothing to do with
the design of an artificial fly at all. It had originally meant
using a fly straight from the fly wallet or fly box and
substituting this dry fly, which being dry would float, for a fly
that had become soaked and was sinking. The words 'dry fly'
were first used in a small pocket textbook on flyfishing by
George Pulman of Axminster in1841:

> So, as it is not in the nature of things that this soaked artificial
> fly can swim upon the surface like the natural ones do, it
> follows the alternative and sinks below the rising fish, the notice
> of which it entirely escapes, because they happen to be looking
> upwards for the material of their meal. Let a dry fly be
> substituted for the wet one, the line switched a few times
> through the air to throw off the superabundant moisture, a
> judicious cast made just above the rising fish, and the fly
> allowed to float towards and over them, and the chances are ten
> to one it will be seized as readily as the living insect.

So, purely by chance, the new word caught on. It was so much easier and simpler to say 'dry fly' rather than 'floating fly' which was how it had been described before. Moreover the new phrase - fishing the dry fly - had an evocative appeal that fishing the floater lacked. Pulman was of course drying the line and not the fly - that was already dry, having come fresh from his wallet - which suggests that he was using either a silk line or a silk and hair line, both of which would absorb water, and not a horsehair line which is not absorbent, as we have seen. However, Pulman deserves a minor immortality for having introduced that one word 'dry'.

Purely by chance, Marryat met F. M. Halford at Hammonds tackle shop in Winchester which led to the setting up of a remarkable partnership. It is worth looking at these two men for they had a considerable influence on the future of fishing.

George Selwyn Marryat (1840-1896) was born at Mapperton Manor in Dorset in southern England and went to Winchester School. He came from a military family and after leaving school became a lieutenant in the 6th Dragoon Guards with whom he served abroad, mostly in India. He retired early at the age of thirty, came back to live in Dorset and Hampshire, and spent the next 26 years of his life mostly fishing and tying flies. He became very knowledgeable and efficient at both and Viscount Grey - then Sir Edward Grey - who also fished the upper Itchen, described Marryat as 'the finest fisherman in England'. Marryat, a retiring personality, would have found that embarrassing.

Frederic M. Halford (1844-1915) was a very different personality and not in the least retiring. He came from a rich family and for most of his life did not need to work. He began as a bait fisherman but had the chance of fishing the fly on the Wandle, a chalkstream near London, where he was advised to fish the dry fly which was known as 'the Carshalton dodge'. He did so and then had the chance of fishing on the Test and became fascinated by the dry fly. He did not know a great deal about flyfishing at that stage but when he met Marryat in John Hammond's shop in The Square at Winchester - and he would have known of Marryat's reputation - he asked him questions about flydressings and Marryat answered as best he could.

Halford later asked Marryat to fish with him on the Test and after some time was so impressed with his knowledge that he suggested that Marryat might join him in a scientific study of fly dressings, the natural fly and its imitation, methods of fishing, and tackle and technique. Marryat agreed and Halford took rooms at Bossington Mill just below the Houghton water on the Test and they worked together for six years. Their joint studies resulted in the publication in 1886 under Halford's name of his first book, *Floating Flies and How to Dress Them*.

Halford asked Marryat to have both their names as the authors but Marryat refused. After the publication of the book under Halford's name alone the two men - according to local gossip - saw very little of each other. One would have thought it was not a natural reticence on Marryat's part, more a conflict of opinion or personality, which was the cause of the breach.

We do not know. But two things are significant. Marryat was not exclusively a dry fly man. A fly box of his which I happened to see at one time contained many traditional wet flies. Halford was all for a dry-fly-only code on the chalkstreams. Indeed one of Halford's followers was to write later:

> Halford...considered that the dry fly had superseded for all time and in all places all other methods of fly fishing and those who thought otherwise were either ignorant or incompetent.
>
> (J. Waller Hills)

Marryat was a dedicated dry fly man, but he was also fond of using the sunk fly in certain conditions. An intolerant attitude of one of the partners in the enterprise might well have led to the break.

So far as I can judge Marryat's character he was the kind of man who did not particularly like argument or dissension, nor would he have wanted to be involved in what we might call the politics of the dry fly, the establishment of a universal dry fly code of practice which would replace all other methods of fishing on the chalkstreams. We do not know for certain because all those who were involved at the time kept silent.

For whatever reason, however, Halford's books gained worldwide approval and Marryat sank, I suspect happily, into the background.

CHAPTER ELEVEN

Halford

Halford has been called the historian of the dry fly (Waller Hills) and the high priest of the dry fly (Overfield). High priest seems more satisfactory, it seems to match better his character, or what one judges of his character from his writing: a rigid discipline, a meticulous exact imitation of the natural insect, even using the right coloured silk to represent its eyes and an almost evangelical attitude towards the dissemination of the cult of the dry fly.

During his life time he was highly praised as the acknowledged leader of chalkstream fishing, and from his seven books the idea of the dry fly spread throughout the land and ultimately the world. He was a colossus of his time. Nothing can take away from the magnitude of his achievements. Perhaps it is even possible that the height he reached in the estimation of chalkstream fishermen may have encouraged the reactions which led to the diminution of his reputation by the generations that were to follow.

High priests have naturally to face the odium of those of a different faith and this is what happened to Halford. He starts off his best-known book, *Dry Fly Fishing in Theory and Practice* (1889), by paying a fulsome tribute to wet fly fishermen - 'the skill exhibited by the experienced and intelligent followers of the wet fly 'and in the rest of the book criticises the wet fly as being of no real value whatever on the chalkstreams where it did not have 'the smallest chance against the dry'.

He rubs it in too. He is contemptuous of a man he calls 'a great Scotch fisher', who is probably W. C. Stewart, 'who thinks he can do well with the wet fly on the chalkstreams,' but such 'obstinate people' soon learn that their infallible systems do not work with the dainty over-fed fish of the chalk.

Halford has a case, of course, but typically it is overstated and that diminishes its value and its effect. Fishermen on the northern rivers of England, rivers that spring from the limestone and freestone hills, the tumbling spate rivers, find that there are times when the dry fly is not so effective as the traditional way of fishing - two or three flies on a leader cast upstream into the food stream when there are no fish rising. The fisherman wades upstream, casting a short line on a long rod - ten foot perhaps - into likely places, letting the tail fly sink, keeping the bob fly as near as possible on the surface. Halford's condemnation of this method and of Stewart had no effect on northern fishermen. They merely thought he was rather stupid, a conceited southerner who did not know what he was talking about.

Halford was not a good writer and there are also times when he exudes subservience. Instead of saying that he was given a day's fishing by a friend he says it was given to him 'by a nobleman residing within a short distance of the metropolis', not entirely an endearing phrase. Then of course, there was this:

> Those of us who will not in any circumstances cast except over rising fish are sometimes called ultra purists and those who occasionally will try to tempt a fish in position but not actually rising are termed purists... and I would urge every dry fly fisher to follow the example of these purists and ultra purists.

Frederic M. Halford, the 'eminence grise' of the dry fly

This over-fastidious use of language was a pity because it masked Halford's achievements. They were indeed great. In a foreword to a centenary edition of *Dry Fly Fishing in Theory and Practice*, Dermot Wilson points out that many of the things which are said about dry fly fishing in books and magazines of today had been discussed by Halford as long ago as 1889, and that

> the true value of the book is reflected by its overwhelming fascination as the harbinger of an entirely new era in the history of fly fishing, the era in which every one of us lives today. It is the era in which the importance of entomology is at last fully appreciated. It is also, in spite of the addition of effective nymphs to our armoury, the era of the dry fly.

Halford is very good on tactics which is not surprising. Many of his ideas may have come from the greater experience of Marryat: how to put a fly to a difficult fish, the ways of rivers, rivercraft and the habits of trout. There is for the first time a detailed description of how a dry fly can be fished downstream:

> Some natural obstruction on the bank or an extremely long throw may render the underhand cast difficult, or even impossible; or on rare occasions too the force of the downstream wind may be too great to be overcome. In either of these cases the fisherman must place himself directly opposite to or slightly above where the fish is feeding. The ordinary overhead cast must then be made, or if necessary, owing to the distance being very great, the steeple cast is used, and with either of them a slight downward cut is incorporated, and at the moment that the fly has travelled out the full extent of the line the cast is perceptibly checked and the fly lands on the water with the last yard of the gut straight, and the remainder of the gut and a portion of the reel line in curves or loosely behind it. At the moment that the fly touches the water the hand is

lowered to allow it to come over the fish before the line is sufficiently taut to cause a drag, and ... sometimes it is necessary for the angler to walk at the same pace and in the same direction as the fly is floating down.

This is a valued technique though not one that is used much on the chalkstreams today. But it is used in America where they have developed what is known as the 'reach cast' where line is fed to the fly through the rod rings by the sideway movement of the rod.

Halford is very good in describing many ways of avoiding drag. Among them, this:

Fish, more especially grayling, often rise in a smooth place immediately above a swift run, and in such a position a straight cast made up-stream from below lays the reel line on the fastest of the run, and the fly, being on the comparatively still glide above, is dragged down by it. To avoid this drag, the place must either be fished from above with the half-drift, or from below with a good deal of slack line on the run so that the fly is below the fish before it commences to drag.

Halford became a little more rigid, more opinionated, as he aged and had the reputation of being the *eminence grise* of the dry fly. You may remember that he gave up using the Gold-Ribbed Hare's Ear because he could not decide what natural fly it was intended to represent. In a way, believing as he did, this was no doubt a logical decision for him to take. In his early days it was different:

The stream was beautifully clear and flowed at a fair pace. The only flies visible seemed to be iron blues, of which here and there an occasional specimen was floating down, not appreciated by the trout. At length one close to the opposite bank was taken, then another, then a third. The fish rose

G. E. M. Skues: 'father of the nymph'

immediately under the bough of an alder overhanging not more than a foot above the surface. The artificial on the cast was a starling-winged hare's ear, the body ribbed with flat gold; to my great delight I succeeded at the first attempt.

He took four brace on the Gold-Ribbed Hare's Ear and having returned as many more he gave up fishing and:

During the whole time no fly except iron blues were seen and yet every one of the fish hooked or killed took the gold-ribbed hare's ear which by no possible stretch of the imagination can be considered an imitation of the blueish-tinged wings and purple body of the iron blue.

Halford became an uncompromising opponent of the nymph, yet when he comes to the problem of trout which are 'bulging', that is, feeding on nymphs under water and making a bulging rise as they do so, he suggests that

probably the best fly to use is the *gold-ribbed hare's ear* [his italics] and the reason is not far to seek. Put side by side under a microscope... a nymph of any of the Ephemeridae and an artificial of the above pattern... and it will be seen that the branchiae of the nymph bears a very strong resemblance to the short hairs of the fur picked out in the body of the artificial.

He established a simple creed. It was comprehensive and precise. It applied to the chalkstreams but it had far wider implications. Consciously or unconsciously we all follow it today:

Dry fly fishing is presenting to the rising fish the best possible imitation of the insect on which he is feeding in its natural position. To analyse this further, it is necessary, firstly to find a fish feeding on the winged insect; both as to size and colour;

thirdly, to present it to him in its natural position or floating on the surface of the water with its wings up, or what we technically term 'cocked'; fourthly, to put the fly lightly on the water, so that it floats accurately over him without drag; and, fifthly, to take care that all these conditions have been fulfilled before the fish has seen the angler or the reflection of his rod.

It could not be improved upon. For the first time it described with a meticulous precision exactly what the dry fly fisherman had to do at every stage of his presentation to the fish. This was the first true gospel of the dry fly and its disciples ever since have followed it humbly, happily and without question as a perfection of the art. As it was in the 1880s, so now:

I know that trout can be caught with a worm, or a maggot, by spinning, wet fly fishing, or nymph fishing, and I knew that at times these methods will catch more fish than any other. I have no objection whatsoever to anglers practising these methods to their heart's content. As for myself I am not particularly interested in killing trout. What does interest me immensely is catching trout by a method we call dry fly, a method that is so intriguing, so full of perplexities and uncertainties, that the actual capture of the fish fades into insignificance compared to the mental stimulation involved. Therefore, I fish where this method is practised exclusively, where I can converse with others who think as I do on problems of mutual interest.

(David Jacques, *Fisherman's Fly*, 1969)

CHAPTER TWELVE

Branche Line

Halford's dry fly code spread to many countries throughout the world, though with modifications and in many cases improvements. He made the mistake of designing his flies by looking down on the natural insect and making an effort to imitate it exactly as it appeared to the human eye. But the trout, looking up at the fly as it imprinted itself on the water window against a background of the sky, was seeing something that was very different from Halford's artificials. Moreover, the condition of chalkstream water is by no means the same as those of other rivers. Chalkstreams are placid waters with an even flow. Other rivers have very different flows and hatching duns can have very different habits.

In the United States, Theodore Gordon (1854-1915) who corresponded with Halford, designed flies that were more suited to the insects that inhabited his freestone rivers and spring creeks. In Scotland, on the Borders, H. B. McCaskie found that the chalkstream flies were too bushy and that more lightly-built patterns were necessary on rivers like the Tweed, Whitewater and Jed. On some of the rivers in the north of England the dry fly was not all that satisfactory because the habit of the hatching fly on rivers such as the Wharfe bears little or no relationship with their behaviour on the chalkstreams where you often get a drift of the sub-imago of many yards. On the Wharfe, and no doubt on other rivers, for some reason which is still to be explained, the dun will pull itself out to the nymphal shuck and take to the air almost at once. There is practically no drift at all.

A definition of the principle of the dry fly had been established after intensive studies on the chalkstreams but considerable adjustments had to be made in practice for other rivers, not to the principle itself, but to the way in which it was applied. This was particularly true, to take one example, on fast, ruffled, shallow streams where the flow might be at least twice as fast as on the chalk.

A surgeon who fished the Devon streams, H. C. Cutcliffe, had earlier (in 1863) given some idea of the upstream fly method on fast waters. He used hackled flies fished either on or just below the surface. The flies, he instructed, must have hackles of a brilliant lustre from game cocks, a hare's flex body with a gold twist and a rusty red hackle. It was not important to imitate the natural fly as both natural and artificial flies were coming down the stream so fast that it did not matter. He used two or three flies of different appearance on a cast and if the flies were to sink you had to strike on the turn of the trout. It was not exactly dry fly, more like Stewart's methods on the Borders. It was similar to the method used by Thaddeus Norris and described in his *American Anglers Book in 1864*.

Not long after Halford's death in 1914, another American, George La Branche, gave trout fishermen on both sides of the Atlantic ways of coping with fishing the dry fly on rapid streams - in fact that was virtually the title of his book. I must confess a weakness for La Branche as I have for Stewart. There is no authoritarian you-must-do-as-I-say attitude about him at all. Not at all. La Branche said that he liked fishing with winged flies not because they might look more natural to the trout but simply because they looked more natural to him, and then went on to admit quite openly that it was quite possible

*Theodore Gordon corresponded with Halford and introduced
the dry fly and the nymph to America*

that hackled flies might be better than winged. That is the kind
of fly fisherman I like, relaxed and civilised.

La Branche emphasised in his book, *The Dry Fly and Fast
Water*, that the presentation of the fly was more important than
the pattern. This meant he had some influence in Britain and in
his home country he was regarded as having created a
distinctly American school of the dry fly.

He did not disagree with the idea of having a fair imitation
of the natural insect but thought that the imitation of its form,

its shape, was quite as essential as colour, and frequently the size of the artificial would be found to be even more important than either. But it was the way in which his flies were fished, the presentation, which was revolutionary.

He gives many examples. He was fishing a pool which was about six feet deep and very clear. There was a large brown trout on the bottom. After six casts the trout lifted a little. He went on casting. The fly came down over the fish again and again, as many as 25 times. By then the fish was within six inches of the surface but refused to take. The next time the fly came over it the fish followed it down and took. That was probably on a stream where the fish had not seen a dry fly before. But the same kind of approach worked well on heavily fished streams in New York State and Pennsylvania. He was known to have fished no more than a hundred yards of river in four hours. His philosophy was to keep on casting:

> Ask him to come to the fly and while he may seem diffident at first he will finally accept the invitation.

Repeated casting in the same place in the food stream does pay but of course it does depend on how many trout are likely to be there, indeed if any trout are there at all. Nevertheless, time and again he was able to say that after many refusals, eventually a trout would rise. He would 'force a rise'. When I tried out his method on the Yorkshire becks, repeated casting did bring up fish which I had not expected to be there. It was a new weapon in the armoury of the dry fly. La Branche - and this is the charm of the man - was by no means dogmatic about it:

> It is not my purpose to contend that the dry fly is more effective than the wet fly though I do believe that under certain conditions the dry fly will take fish that may not be taken in any other manner. I do contend however that a greater fascination attends its use.

But a moderate opinion of that kind was no longer possible on the chalkstreams of Hampshire which within a few years of Halford's second book - about the mid 1890s - were the scene of great conflict over the counter-revolution of the wet fly led by a London lawyer, G. E. M. Skues. It was a sad period in flyfishing history and created a good deal of bitterness and unhappiness.

To understand the conflict one must realise that until the sudden arrival of the dry fly - the floater - most of the fishing on the chalkstreams had been blowline fishing with the natural insect - the big mayfly - or wet fly downstream. Each year, after about June, all fishing more or less ceased as the weed growth was too thick for fly or bait. Weed cutting, which started erratically after World War I, introduced the potential for flyfishing throughout the season, but until this practice became prevalent, fishing the fly was limited to those early-season times when the duns were hatching or the spinners falling. At other times, except in the big mayfly season, the water would be unfishable if the trout were hunting in the remaining thick weed beds for shrimp and snail.

So the arrival of the dry fly on this type of river was quite revolutionary. It was seized upon with delight for it meant far more fishing could be done with a fly that was floating over the surface of the water even if there were thick weeds not far below.

Before the dry fly arrived very few chalkstream fishermen were aware that even before the arrival of the split-wing floater and the double split-wing floater, their ancestors on the other rivers had been fishing upstream. They had always been seeking techniques which would give a longer float than was possible with their fairly primitive patterns. The chalkstream fishermen did not seem to have read Stewart about the way to fish the floating dropper on the Border rivers, they did not seem to have read Scotcher and certainly hardly anyone was aware of Venables. Consequently, the impact of the dry fly on the chalkstreams was far greater than it was on some of the limestone streams and the Border rivers where floating fly fishing was a technique that was well known though not ever easy to acquire.

We have several accounts of the astonishment and enthusiasm that the floating fly engendered among chalkstream fishermen at that time. Plunket Greene, the concert singer, who fished the Bourne where it flows into the Test, saw his first dry flies fished while on holiday in Germany:

> The Wildbad river was a wonderful trout stream. We used to get plenty of pounders and one-and-a-half-pounders on Zulus and March Browns...but [one day] we saw a man in salmon waders standing in the middle of the mill pool in the town casting upstream with something invisible to the naked eye and just as we came abreast of him he suddenly for our especial benefit got fast into something between a torpedo and a whale and after a grand battle landed a four-pound trout. The fisherman was Mr Stephen Rawson for whose long life and happiness I shall ever pray for he inoculated me there and then with the dry fly cult and all the fun I have had since then I owe to the first lessons he gave me.

Greene was quite right to use the word cult because on some of the chalkstreams the dry fly became an article of faith, a belief that was as strong or sometimes possibly even stronger than the most deep-seated convictions that could be experienced within noticeable distance of a religion. It was therefore not in the least surprising that the dry fly was supreme and the wet fly no longer of any value on the chalk, only perhaps on other, lesser, rivers.

The affection for the dry fly was paramount because it was far more effective in taking fish on the chalkstreams than any other method that had been tried before. Exuberant praise, for example, was lavished by Plunket Greene on the winged Iron Blue, which

> always seems to me to be happier and keener and to have better manners than all the rest. He is an aristocrat, a prince on the wing, far above the world of underwater hacklers, as he sails down serene on the stream, oblivious to wind or rain or the sun, above board in his every thought, ready to work for you again and again till he disintegrates and falls to pieces from very exhaustion.

But while the chalkstream fishermen of Hampshire were enjoying themselves in that halcyon part of the world, many of the good trout and salmon rivers in England and South Wales were either dead or dying.

CHAPTER THIRTEEN

Reservoirs of Poison

Towards the latter part of the 18th century and during the whole of the 19th the nature of our rivers changed. They no longer 'teemed with fish' as they had done in Izaak Walton's time. Gradually, in some rivers, and very rapidly in others, the quality of the water began to depend entirely on the concentration of human activity along the banks. With more people, new towns and new industries, rivers began to be used as drains and sewers. They were being systematically poisoned. Fish and insect life was being destroyed.

It seemed natural at the time to use rivers to carry away the effluent from the growing number of tanneries, factories of all kinds, textile mills, iron foundries and coal mines which were established along the river valleys in what historians were to call 'the headlong change' of the industrial revolution.

The demands on the new methods of mass production were enormous: weapons to defeat Napoleon, woollen and cotton cloth for overseas trade, and to meet all the demands of the growth of empire and the colonies. In a matter of fifty years the population had doubled and the new industrial conurbations created an enormous tonnage of human waste which went into the rivers.

It is difficult for us to realise what appalling damage was done to the entire environment by what Blake was to call 'these dark satanic mills'. We still have the phrase 'the black country' to remind us what it was like. There were thick smogs from the blast furnaces and the factory chimneys. Houses and streets were covered in soot. The sun was obscured for weeks at a time. Thousands died from diseases caused by breathing the polluted air and drinking poisoned water. Thousands died in the great cholera outbreaks of 1832 and 1848.

The river Aire was a lovely trout stream which rose in limestone country near Malham Tarn in North Yorkshire but this is what happened to it when it got to the city of Leeds, then a manufacturing town, in West Yorkshire:

> The Aire [is] a reservoir of poison kept for the breeding of a pestilence in the town [and] was indeed composed of a disgusting array of lethal ingredients. It was full of refuse from water closets, cesspools, privies, common drains, dunghill drainings, infirmary refuse, wastes from slaughter houses, chemical soap, gas, dye houses and manufacturers, coloured blue and black dye, pig manure, old urine wash; and there were dead animals, vegetable substances and occasionally a decomposing body.
>
> (*Public Health in Leeds*, Wohl Toft, 1840)

The rivers most likely to have been grossly affected by pollution were those draining the textile areas of Yorkshire and Lancashire and the inland engineering areas of South Yorkshire and the Midlands. Rivers in the South Wales coalfields were also badly polluted. This would affect to a varying extent something like five to eight thousand miles of waterways including the lower reaches of the Thames where the salmon runs ended around 1820. This was as a result of the heavy pollution of the docks and of sewage from above Westminster where 'the disgusting smells of excrement from the river' prevented members of Parliament taking tea on the terrace of the Parliament buildings.

110

Concern about pollution and public health resulted in no less than 22 reports from Royal Commissions between 1816 and 1915 and during that time no less than three Acts of Parliament were passed for the control of pollution but the effective clauses of the Acts were not proceeded with because of the damage they might cause to industry. The pollution of Leeds, bad enough in 1840, was even worse in 1867:

> The rivers Aire and Calder and their tributaries are abused by passing into them hundreds of thousands of tons per annum of ashes, slag, cinders from steel boiler furnaces, iron works and domestic fires; by their being made the receptacle of broken pottery and worn-out utensils of metal, refuse brick from brickyards and old buildings, earth, stone, and clay from quarries and excavations; road scraping, street sweeping, etc; by spent dyewoods and other solids used in the treatment of worsteds and woollens; by hundred of carcases of animals, such as dogs, cats, pigs, etc. which are allowed to float on the surface of the streams or putrify on their banks; and by the flowing in, to the amount of many, very many, millions of gallons a day, of water poisoned, corrupted and clogged by refuse from mines, chemical works, dyeing, scouring and fulling worsted and woollen stuffs, skin cleansing and tannery, slaughter house garbage and sewage from houses and the town.
>
> *(Report of the Royal Commission on River Pollution, 1867)*

On many rivers pollution continued completely unchecked. The Tees on the North East coast was killed as a salmon river in the 1920s by petrochemical and steel industries situated along the estuary.

> Early this century [on the Tees] the annual catch of salmon was nearly 8,000 fish; owing to pollution this had dropped by 1930-34 to 2,000. In 1937 only 23 fish were caught whilst by 1950

111

there were no salmon at all...Another impressive example is the Tyne estuary where extensive pollution caused catches of salmon to drop from 868,000 lbs in 1873 to a mere 2,200 lbs in 1960.

(River Pollution, Louis Klein, 1966)

It was only in the late 1980s and early 1990s that efforts were made to prevent further pollution. In 1989 a National Rivers Authority, partly funded by Government, was set up to be the 'guardian of the water environment'. Industrial and agricultural organisations protested against the extent of some of the penalties imposed upon polluters by the Authority in the first two years of its existence. It remains to be seen how effective the NRA may be.

In the 1870s and 1880s, some of the public water supply reservoirs were opened for angling. The best example of this was in Sheffield in Yorkshire where the local river was 'a mass of ink and stink'. Members of the Sheffield anglers' club had nowhere to fish. One of the water supply reservoirs in the hills above the town was opened 'for the relaxation of the working class'. The reservoir was full of small wild brown trout which had spawned in one of the feeder streams.

Within a year or so the local fishermen, using maggot and worm, had emptied the reservoir of fish. It was restocked with hatchery trout from Loch Leven, shelters were built, and the price of day tickets increased from one shilling to two-and-sixpence. Other cities followed Sheffield's example though one or two, such as Manchester, put restrictions on the use of maggots and groundbaiting in reservoirs that supplied the public with drinking water. Apart from this 'any legitimate form of angling' was allowed. Worm fishing was the most popular. That was the start of reservoir trout fishing.

This sequence of flies covers a period of about 1600 years. The top row suggests how the Macedonians might have tied their flies while the second row follows the patterns rather vaguely described by Juliana Berners. Cotton and Barker's flies and Venables' upside-down fly (third row) show a slightly more elaborate approach. Bowlker's Green Drake and Blue Dun (bottom row) are in effect the first of the moderns.

PIONEER RESERVOIR PATTERNS

Three midge patterns tied by Dr Bell of Blagdon

Three nymph patterns also tied by Dr Bell

Metal wobbler   Halcyon spinning vane

Minnow fly

Black & peacock spider   Green/yellow nymph   Green nymph

Dr Bell's nymphs were the forerunners of the many imitative nymph patterns in use today. The two metal minnows (third row) were banned under the fly-only rule. This prompted anglers to invent Minnow flies and a myriad of reservoir lures. Tom Ivens (see bottom row) devised some enduring representations of underwater insects.

DEVELOPMENT OF HAIRWING SALMON FLIES

Single hook hairwing   Double hook hairwing

Tube fly   Salmon bug

The Waddington   Tandem Evelyn lure

Simple hairwing flies (top row) began to take the place of the feather-winged patterns of the Kelson era. In the 1950s came the first tube flies (second row, left) and Waddington's articulated-hook dressings (bottom row, left) took the design a stage further still. Long lures became popular with both salmon and seatrout anglers (see Evelyn's tandem lure), but treble hooks were banned in some countries.

THE FEATHER-WING AND DRY SALMON FLIES

The 'monstrous' Horse Leach

Bowlker's Dragon Fly

The Parson

The Golden Butterfly

The Popham

The Black Doctor

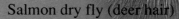

Salmon dry fly (deer hair)

The earliest salmon flies (top row) were probably simple dressings like these. The Irish then developed flamboyant patterns (second row) in the early 1800s, and these in turn inspired the complex multi-winged patterns (third row) so loved by Kelson and his contemporaries. The dry fly was designed for salmon by the American angler Harry Darbee.

DRY FLIES, NYMPHS, SPIDERS AND MAYFLIES

Hall's split-wing floater   Skues' nymph   Sawyer's pheasant tail nymph

No-hackle fly   Black ant   Parachute fly

Three spider patterns

Fan-wing mayfly   Grey Wulff   Shadow mayfly

Certain flies can justifiably claim their place in history (top row). Typical of American inventiveness are Swisher and Richards' No-hackle fly and MacMurray's Black ant. The 'parachute' style originated in Scotland but is popular on both sides of the Atlantic. The spiders of the North Country and Scottish Borders (third row) were in use as long ago as the mid-1700s. The Victorian Fan-wing Mayfly looks convincing enough to us, but chalkstream fishers nowadays prefer the 'impressionistic' hairwing Wulff patterns or the Deane Shadow Mayfly, designed from the fish's perspective.

PLATE FROM SCOTCHER'S *FLY FISHER'S LEGACY*

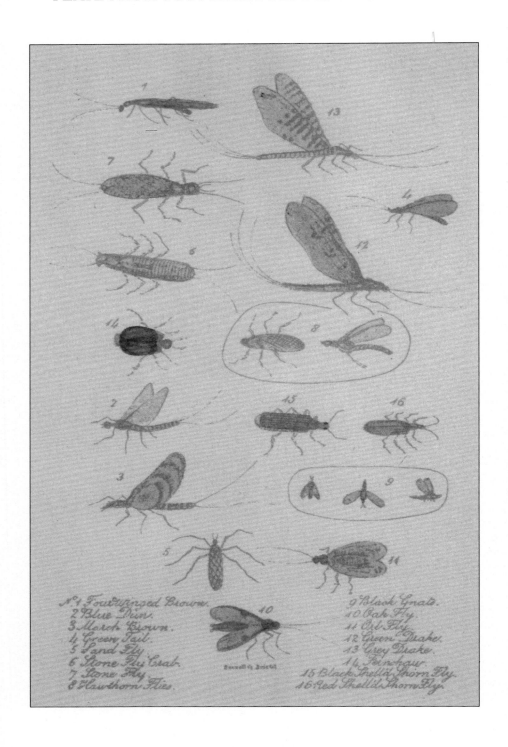

N° 1 Four winged Brown.
2 Blue Dun.
3 March Brown.
4 Green Tail.
5 Sand Fly.
6 Stone Fly Crab.
7 Stone Fly.
8 Hawthorn Flies.

9 Black Gnats.
10 Oak Fly.
11 Orl Fly.
12 Green Drake.
13 Grey Drake.
14 Peinchaw.
15 Black Shell'd Thorn Fly.
16 Red Shell'd Thorn Fly.

PLATE FROM KELSON'S *THE SALMON FLY*

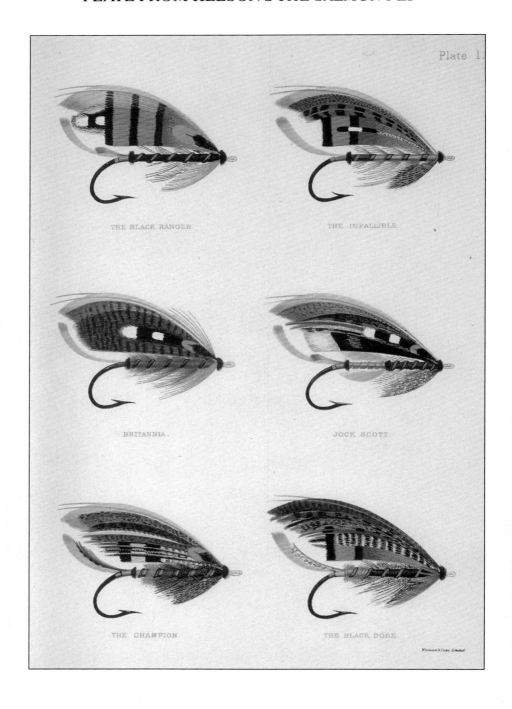

CHAPTER FOURTEEN

The Nymph Men

Pollution destroyed some of the London chalkstreams, notably the Wandle where Lord Nelson had fished the fly on his estate at Mitcham in Surrey, but the chalkstreams of the Salisbury Downs - of Berkshire, Wiltshire and Hampshire - were safe for Halford to carry out his experiments at Bossington on the Test, and for his opponent, G. E. M. Skues, known as 'father of the nymph' to explore the possibility of the upstream wet fly on the Itchen.

George Edward Mackenzie Skues (1858-1949) was a London lawyer and at the start of his career as a fisherman he fished only the dry fly on the Abbots Barton water, above Winchester, where he was a member of the syndicate for 56 years.

Skues was an accurate observer and he noticed that when, at times, he put on a fly that sank by chance, the trout sometimes took it in preference to a floater. This went against all his beliefs and training as a dry fly fisherman. He described what happened in magazine articles - he was a prolific writer - and ultimately his articles were collected in book form. His first and most important book was *Minor Tactics of the Chalk Stream* (1910).

In this he described how on one muggy September day in 1892 the trout were rising, or so he thought, to take the winged fly on the surface, but had refused all his offers. In despair he put on a hen-hackled Blue Dun which became waterlogged and sank and was at once taken. He was quite astonished but continued to fish with it as a wet fly cast upstream to the rises. It took two more trout.

He began to experiment with wet flies and ultimately, after he had explored the stomach contents of trout with a marrow spoon, he tied flies to imitate the nymphs which they had been eating. His artificials were unweighted and to make them sink a little below the surface he used glycerine or wetted them with saliva. They were suggestions of the nymphs that were to be found close to the surface.

Skues then put forward a system of fishing which included all the stages of the nymphs and flies of the ephemeroptera. First came the arrival of the nymphs, their ascent through the water and the ecdysis on the surface, then the float of the sub-imago, and thirdly the aftermath of the hatch when the trout continued to feed again under the water. Skues pointed out that the dry fly man restricted his fishing to only one of these three stages - the float of the duns - but why should he do so if he could fish all three?

It was of course an entirely logical argument but logic is not always a companion to a fisherman. Skues' books and articles raised a storm of protest from the followers of Halford - disciples might have been a better word - for at that time, according to Waller Hills, the dry fly men formed 'an intolerant dictatorship'. It was a pity, and it saddened the rest of Skues' life.

The dry fly man had only to say 'Yes of course, my dear Skues, trout can be taken below the surface of the water in several ways but we just prefer to fish a floating fly on top of the water'; but they wanted something more positive and damning than that. They suggested that Skues was misinformed, that you could not imitate nymphs, you could not imitate their wiggle, that it would be abused by men fishing downstream and catching undersized fish. The debate became very heated.

In fairness, we must remember a little of the background of the time. Until the arrival of the new rods and lines from America - the whipping rods they were called - men on the Test fished the wet fly downstream or used the blowline with the natural mayfly impaled on the hook. Now the new American rods and lines had arrived and the floating flies were taking fish more efficiently than the blowline. Then here comes this man Skues who says the dry fly is no good. How absurd! Not that Skues did actually say that, but that is what they thought he said, and that was enough to put him beyond the pale.

Towards the end of Skues' life he heard from friends about a river keeper on the upper Avon. Frank Sawyer (1907-1980) had developed a new kind of nymph which, instead of being tied with silk or nylon, used fine copper wire so that the

Frank Sawyer, the Avon riverkeeper

115

artificial would sink fast.

The Sawyer nymphs were very simple, merely giving the illusion of a nymph rather than an imitation. The bodies were formed of wire with a pronounced hump for the thorax and were covered with the red fibres from a cock pheasant's tail. There were no legs, no hackle, for these designs suggested the nymphs that were moving under water which had their legs tucked close to their bodies. Skues' nymphs had hackles and were fished inert on a dead drift, almost as if they were dry flies, and today we would call them 'emerger patterns'.

Skues was impressed with Sawyer and was among those who helped to encourage him to write articles and to broadcast. Today, the Sawyer Pheasant Tail Nymph has largely replaced the Skues patterns as it is not only exceptionally effective but is simple and easy to tie.

Fishing the nymph was not entirely new though it was thought so at the time. Various ways of fishing a fly underwater had been tried in the United States in the mid-1800s, mostly using ordinary artificials with a shot on the line. In the 1860s Cutcliffe, the Devon fisherman, suggested imitating what he called the larvae which hatched into flies, though he thought the worm might be more effective.

However, a fairly detailed way of fishing the nymph was described by John Younger in a book published in Kelso in 1840, *River Angling for Salmon and Trout*. Apart from the fact that Younger called a nymph a maggot it was a clear description of the method:

When the flies come quickly on the surface and no trout takes them...then for a trial of skill mutilate the wings of your flies by picking them off about half middle (not cutting them); or rather by tying down the top of the wings to near the tail of the fly which makes it appear something like the maggot released from

116

John Younger: 'mutilate the wings of your flies...'

its first case on the bottom stone and on its ascent to the surface. Then as much as you can let them sink low in the water, altogether below those flies on the surface, and you will most likely succeed in getting a few trouts.

The 1840 copy of Younger's book, now in the Flyfishers' Club library in London, is one that belonged to Skues.

CHAPTER FIFTEEN

Bell's Bugs

Skues and Sawyer were to have a considerable influence on the techniques and the approach to upstream wet fly fishing of many fishermen in many countries, but the interesting thing so far as stillwater fishing was concerned was the effect they had on the English reservoirs, especially when one remembers that Skues' nymphs were the products of the chalkstreams, and were intended to be fished only on the chalkstreams as an adjunct to the fly.

Trout fishing in reservoirs began about 1870-1880. It was mostly bait fishing to begin with - the worm was the most popular bait - but now and again a flyfisherman might try his hand, though most of them had no idea what kind of flies to use. H. T. Sheringham, angling editor of *The Field*, was attracted to the newly-opened lake of Blagdon in Somerset in 1904 as a result of the phenomenal catches there. He fished salmon flies but suspected they were too large and thought that reservoirs needed new patterns.

Then came the man who supplied them. Howard Alexander Bell, a doctor, was one of the few men who survived the terrible battles of Passchendaele and Third Ypres in the First World War. He worked among the injured and dying at one of the forward dressing stations and, like so many, what he saw and endured had a lasting effect. When he came back to England after the Armistice he took up a country practice in

119

Sussex. He was looked upon as a good doctor but a bit odd, very reserved, morose, not wanting to have any social contact with anybody. The horrors of Flanders had gone deep.

He took up flyfishing, probably as a therapy, and from about 1920 onwards fished at Blagdon reservoir in Somerset on any weekend that he could get away from his practice. At some point in the early 1920s he bought Skues' book - *Minor Tactics* - and, following Skues' advice to find out what trout were eating, he examined the contents of their stomachs with the method that the author had recommended, the use of a marrow spoon. 'He would have spooned out his grandmother if he thought there'd be anything in her' quipped the local police constable, himself one of the Blagdon regulars.

Bell tied artificials to represent the insects that he found in the Blagdon trout, including bloodworms, midge and sedge pupae and beetles. There was not a winged fly to be seen. In the 1930s he was able to buy a practice at Wrington, not far from the lake, and opened a surgery in Blagdon itself, just up the hill. By now Bell had a reputation as a great fisherman. He was always taking trout when others were blank. Gradually his imitative patterns became known.

My maternal grandfather, Willie Cox, who fished Blagdon at that time called them 'Bell's Bugs' and he and some others who were fishing Greenwells and Mallards thought it was not sporting to fish imitation bait. A friend of Bell's, Eric Newsom, describes Bell's methods of fishing, and as this was probably the first time that imitative patterns had been fished on reservoirs it is worth giving the details:

> Bell would always go off on his own, trying to avoid other rods. He had a pear-shaped landing net slung over his shoulder on a cord. He always fished from the bank with three unweighted flies on a gut cast, size 1X. He liked to fish over sunk ditches

and holes and weed beds. He moved slowly along the bank, casting as he went. He cast out as far as was comfortable. He made no attempt to go for distance but let the flies sink slowly, judging the time so that the tail fly did not get snagged on the bottom. He used the knot at the end of his greased silk line as a bite indicator. When the flies were fully sunk he would gather them in slowly.

His flies were quite small, 10s, 12s, sometimes 14s. He might have a Worm Fly on a single hook on the point, a Grenadier (caddis pupa) on the middle dropper and a Buzzer (midge pupa) on the top. All his dressings were very plain and simple.

He gained a local reputation and then a national one. There were articles about his imitation bait patterns in the *Fishing Gazette* and *The Field*. His friend Eric Newsom showed him *The Field* article and Bell reacted in fury and tore it up then and there. In his latter years he had become even more secretive and morose. My grandfather would say 'You could hardly get a word out of him'. Nevertheless in the 1920s and 30s he set the scene and pointed the way in which imitative patterns of underwater insects were to develop as one of the major techniques of reservoir trout fishing. The new flies had arrived. They were very soon in demand.

CHAPTER SIXTEEN

The Legitimate Method

B ell's bugs were not only in demand from fishermen. They were needed by the accountants of the water companies and water boards who were suddenly horrified at the huge catches of trout in public water supply reservoirs which came from the new and perfectly legitimate angling method of threadline fishing.

This new method of spinning - all methods of spinning were allowed - arrived as a result of the invention of the fixed-spool reel by Arthur Holden Illingworth in 1905. The first models came on the market but were not immediately popular because of various complications in use. However, model No.5 was much better and much simpler to use. It was made popular by Arthur Wanless in the 1930s who designed special light-line rods for use with it, together with very light lines that were perfect for the fixed-spool reels.

The effect on reservoir fishing was devastating. Spinning was a perfectly legitimate method of angling, and this was spinning, but it was also an enormously efficient method of doing so. A beginner could easily cast a bait with the threadline for 40 or 50 yards and fish it at any depth.

Catches rocketed. Men were coming back with the official limit of eight or twelve fish taken on a threadline whereas before they might have been lucky to get two or three.

The cost of restocking the reservoirs doubled, even trebled.

The accountants were alarmed. They pointed out to the water boards and companies that the public would not tolerate an increase in the water rates or charges purely to subsidise sport. Changes had to be made and after various experiments with costs and catch limits, flyfishing only was decided on. From the point of view of the accountants and the fishery managers it was a wise decision. Flyfishing was much less effective than either the threadline or the worm in taking fish.

There were in some cases violent protests especially among anglers in the Midlands. Many ways were invented, including what came to be called 'feathered spinning', to circumvent the new rules. Imitation minnows were made of rather hard substances known as bakelite, decorated with a feathered back and tail, and called fly-minnows. These could be cast some distance with a fly rod if the braided silk line was coiled on the ground.

Devices of this kind came to an end, more or less, with the call up of many reservoir fishermen for national service for the war against Hitler. Even so, there were still anxieties about making the fly-only rule. In the spring of 1943, the general manager of Bristol Waterworks, W. A. D. Alexander, who was responsible for fishing at Blagdon, wrote to a friend, Colonel J. K. B. Crawford, who was a great fly fisherman:

It did me good to see from the fishing return that you and your Invictas did so well. I am sorry now we did not bar Spinning throughout the season but we have a number of Blagdon enthusiasts who are keen on Spinning and I feared the results of such a ban might be disastrous from the financial point of view, because under War conditions we only just pay our way as it is; however, the good results obtained with the fly-only during the first eight days encourages me to stop Spinning next year. I have just heard that 24 fish were killed by 4 rods, all Spinning,

on Sunday last - sacrilege! Dr Bell was one of the culprits, he
got 6 but a man named Rugg got his limit.

By the time World War II ended most reservoirs had accepted a
fly-only rule though some with reservations, but the flies varied
considerably. Progress was mainly on the Midland reservoirs
where skilled anglers developed new styles and new long
distance casting methods.

The scene was set for a stillwater code of practice which
would provide basic fly patterns and the times and places
where they could be used. This came from a Midland angler,
T. C. Ivens, in a book published in 1952 (*Still Water Fly-
Fishing*) which had the same illuminating effect on the
reservoirs as Halford's works on the chalkstreams.

Ivens gave details of five standard general patterns which
created an impression of certain groups of underwater insects
and which could, by representing the trout's natural food, be
used for deceiving them. He called these 'deceivers' and they
were to be fished slowly.

In contrast, under certain conditions, he advocated the use
of 'attractor' patterns, which normally would be fished fast and
would provoke the trout into a take. Variations on the theme of
these patterns, though not necessarily improvements on them,
have continued to be tied ever since.

A further development of stillwater fishing was the
creation of small privately-owned lakes, often from flooded
gravel pits. These were available, especially to begin with in
southern England, for day ticket or subscription flyfishing for
trout. The pioneering work in fishery management of these
small lakes by Alex Behrendt, at Two Lakes near Romsey
which began in 1948, set the standard for the expansion in
small lake fishing which spread to many parts of the British
Isles, and especially in England, where these lakes are more
numerous than elsewhere.

CHAPTER SEVENTEEN

The American Influence

Once again American inventions had a considerable effect on flyfishing in Britain. The braided silk line and the six-sided split cane rods had made the dry fly possible on the chalkstreams in Victorian times. Now, in the years following World War II, new space age materials, most of them developed in the United States, caused a complete change in the way we fished.

In the 1930s the fly fisherman used a cane rod, silk line and a gut cast. In the 1950s he changed to plastic lines, glass-fibre rods and nylon leaders. For those who experienced the change it was quite astonishing and made fishing so much easier in every way.

The development of plastic flylines in America went ahead with considerable speed. A polyvinyl chloride coating was applied to tapered cores by the Cortland company in the early 1950s. About the same time Scientific Anglers Inc. perfected a way in which the plastic coating could be tapered and the core dispensed with. The breakthrough came with the ability to create lines and parts of lines with different specific gravities. Most of the line could be made to float and the last ten feet or so made to sink so that flies could be fished deeper. Complete lines were made to sink at varying speeds and finally lead-cored lines were produced which sank, in the words of the advertisement, 'like a stone'.

Paul Schullery in *American Fly Fishing* (1987) quotes A. J. McClane saying in the *The Practical Fly Fisherman* (1975) that the new synthetic lines had greatly expanded the art of fly fishing 'from top to bottom'. Indeed it had, especially on English reservoirs where lures and imitation baits could as a result be fished at great depths. In some cases large trout were taken on lead-cored shooting heads 90 feet below the surface. As a result of these inventions the fly rod could now quite easily take over the functions of the bait rod and the spinner.

Glass-fibre rods had a comparatively short innings. A new composite material, carbon-fibre, developed at Britain's aeronautical research centre at Farnborough was taken up by American tackle manufacturers in the early 1970s to produce graphite rods. There were breakage troubles with some of the early ones, but they were lighter and their diameters less than glass-fibre and therefore would cast further with less effort. By the 1980s they were in general use.

An interesting stage was passed through in the late 1970s and early 1980s, during which claims and counter-claims flew among manufacturers about whose rods - graphite or boron - were 'pure' and whose were merely mixtures of fibers and therefore 'not really graphite' or 'not genuine boron'. The best makers soon realised that these three materials - graphite, fiberglass and boron - were often better used in combination than alone, and that fly fishers would be best served by less emphasis on purity and more on practical fishing mechanics.

(Paul Schullery)

The new materials of the space age considerably extended the meaning of the word 'fly'. Flyfishing became fishing with a fly rod instead of the earlier meaning of fishing a fly, a winged insect. Flyfishing for shark in the Caribbean meant fishing a five-inch plastic squid with a trout fly rod. Popper bugs, lead-

128

headed jigs and 'death struggle action' lures were also flies within that context, as were weighted shrimps and cork-bodied snails on English reservoirs. The flexibility in the use of the fly rod overcame the original meaning of fishing a fly. It now meant fishing with a fly rod using whatever lure might be appropriate to the fish and the fishing.

This is not to say that traditional flyfishing was in any way

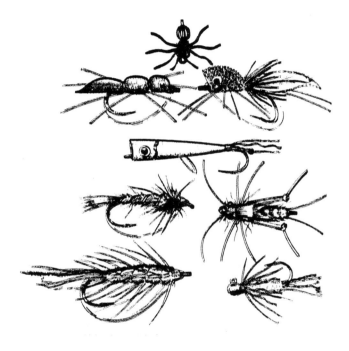

They say we're flies

diminished. On the contrary it became even more than before a distinct and separate art or craft of its own, not by any means as rigid a discipline as it had been under Halford, but more generous-minded and tolerant. For example, the Piscatorial Society, which to begin with had followed the Halford doctrine, relented to the extent that it allowed the use of the unweighted Skues nymphs on its waters as this was a style of fishing 'to be used for trout which can be seen to be feeding at or near the surface yet not taking the dun or its imitation'. It was in a sense, therefore, fishing 'a dry fly style' and could be included in the term 'dry fly'. It did not apply to weighted nymphs.

Traditional loch fishing in Scotland and Ireland made use of the new American tackle - graphite rods and floating plastic lines - but continued otherwise unaffected in the way the lochs had been fished for salmon and trout for an unknown number of centuries.

Dapping the natural mayfly became less popular than it had been, even in Ireland, no doubt on the grounds that it was a cruel practice and that in any case it was just as effective to put on an artificial pattern of a mayfly which could be used for most of the season and was more easily obtainable.

Fishing the drift with a team of wet flies was becoming immensely popular, the flies 'stroking' the water, the bob fly making a 'vee' shape across the waves to attract the fish. This way of fishing has been taken up recently in competitions on English reservoirs by clubs who borrowed the method from Scotland, where it has been used in club matches for as long as anyone can remember.

CHAPTER EIGHTEEN

The Return of the Plume

The Kelson salmon flies faded away with the end of the Victorian era. Scottish flydressers like Wright of Sprouston-on-Tweed (1829-1902) had discovered that dog's hair was just as effective in creating a salmon fly as toucan or macaw, and much cheaper. The Kelson theories about salmon fishing also dissolved in the presence of a new and more rational humility:

> A lifetime of fishing is simply not long enough to learn all there is to know about salmon fishing. There is always more to learn about methods of fishing and about the fish themselves. When a fisherman has caught some 500 salmon he is apt to think that he knows the long and the short of the whole business. With 1500 fish to his rod he begins to be less certain, and by the time he has landed several thousand he has realised he will never get to the bottom of the matter.
> (*A Salmon Fisher's Odyssey*, John Ashley-Cooper, 1982)

Modified Kelson flies with simplified dressings continued to be used in Ireland, in Iceland, in some parts of North America, and among those fishermen in many countries who liked the delicate blends of colour and form of feathers. But the Scots fell in love with a new kind of fly, the tube.

The tube fly was first tied around the year 1945 by Mrs Winnie Morawski of the Charles Playfair tackle company of

Aberdeen. At first she used quill sections of turkey wing feathers with the pith scraped out and on the head of these she tied hair wings. The gut cast was passed through the hollow quill and attached to a small treble.

The Hardy catalogue of 1957 showed tube flies for the first time. By then the tube was plastic but with a separate weighted head, bullet-shaped, and with a hole in it. The nylon was

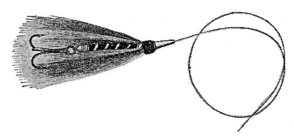

Early tube fly, Hardy catalogue, 1957

threaded through the head, through the tube, and attached to a treble. The Hardy catalogue had a pleasingly descriptive phrase for the dressing:

> In place of wings, hair or hair and feathers are draped around the front of the body like the cover of an umbrella.

The tube fly, and its companion with a metal body and an articulated treble, the Waddington, began to dominate the fishing on most of the big Scottish rivers. It is a charming thought that the tube and the Waddington have close similarities to the Roman plume that was used for rod and line salmon fishing during the Roman occupation of Britain more than 1500 years ago.

The idea of dry fly fishing for salmon in the Scottish rivers was revived for a time without success compared with the rivers of eastern Canada where the dry fly takes something between 30 to 50 per cent of all salmon caught on rod and line. In the province of New Brunswick, and others, it is true dry fly fishing, the fly cast upstream and allowed to drift down without drag in exactly the same way that trout flies are fished. The genetic differences between salmon of the western and the eastern Atlantic are believed to be the reason for the difference of behaviour between the Scottish and the Canadian fish.

At a time when world stocks of salmon had been in decline for something like a quarter of a century, the Canadians took swift action to limit catches. In New Brunswick estuary netting was banned, all salmon over 25 inches taken on rod and line had to be returned to the water by law, and grilse could be kept only to the number of tags issued to anglers. These had to be attached by the guide to the grilse as soon as one was killed. Any untagged fish in the possession of an angler was illegal and the angler liable to a heavy fine. As a result of this action, salmon runs in rivers such as the Miramichi in New Brunswick saw a considerable recovery.

In Scotland, by contrast, no action was taken. An increase in the number of fishermen on Scottish rivers and unrestricted killing caused the Atlantic Salmon Trust, a research body, to issue an appeal to anglers in 1990 to consider returning hen fish to the water to help build up stocks. However, the mood of most fishermen and fishery owners on Scottish rivers was hostile to any idea of catch and release or mandatory control.

The advent of timeshare was unfortunate at this stage for it resulted in what was in effect an encouragement to increase the killing. Timeshare was a method by which anglers could buy named weeks of fishing in perpetuity for the outlay of a capital sum based on catch returns. The temptation for owners to increase the catch returns and thereby the profit on the sale was in many cases irresistible.

The problem was admirably summarised in an article by

Michael Wigan in *The Field* of August, 1991. These were the opening paragraphs:

> The biggest change in the structure of field sports since syndication has been timeshare in salmon fishing. During the Eighties the value of salmon fishing went up by about 12 times, a rise which is explained by the parallel growth of timeshare. Now timeshare is falling into disrepute and may eventually prove to have been an embarrassing cul-de-sac.
>
> The original stimulus for timeshare came from the marketeers. Salmon fishing was viewed as an asset which could be divided up like so many days' pheasant shooting. To inflate catch records, and therefore values, water prepared for sale was intensively fished - with free fishing and bumper prizes - to ensure the water was ploughed up for all it could yield. Then, as if to guarantee a continuation of one season's extraordinary fishing return, managing agents (or selling agents) promised to maintain heavy stocking programmes.

Protests were made. The Atlantic Salmon Trust condemned what it called 'the deplorable behaviour' of a small number of owners and tenants on the lower reaches of the Tay and the Aberdeenshire Dee. The chairman of the Trust, Sir David Nickson, urged fishery boards, which consisted mainly of the owners of fishing, to apply to the Government to ban the use of bait, especially shrimp and prawn, towards the end of the season. He went on:

> All those who have a responsibility for rod fishing have, in my opinion, a duty to ensure that the sport is conducted in a sportsmanlike way and that rod catches are not excessive. The adverse publicity and the effect both on ministerial and public opinion caused by reports from Scotland this autumn [1989] at a

time when both the fish farming industry and the netsmen are under great pressure, has an effect out of all proportion to any damage that may be done to local stocks.

Three fishery boards responded to David Nickson's appeal and applied for a ban on bait towards the end of the season. The Salmon and Trout Association, disturbed at the reports of overkill - 300 salmon were reported from one beat of the Tay in a week - issued a game fishing code which, in effect, urged fishery owners and fishermen to behave like gentlemen.

CHAPTER NINETEEN

A Change of Flies

For most of the 20th century flydressers have been inventing new flies. First of all there was J.C. Mottram in 1914 who was so fascinated by the idea of transparency that he left out most of the body dressing of his Jenny Spinner in an effort to persuade the trout that, as someone said, 'they were looking through a body which wasn't there'. They could still, of course, see the hook shank.

Mottram was interested in spinners. He made one of his olives with a fur body but left out the hackle as he thought legs were unnecessary with spinners. It was a pity his book was published just before World War I as by the end of the war he had been almost forgotten.

Highly commended by Skues, there came Colonel E.W. Harding who carried out many experiments to show that trout flies must be tied from the point of view of the trout, that is from under the water, and not looked down on from above as humans did. Harding was the first to make this point, which now seems obvious, but it was not at the time. Unfortunately he died before he could complete his experiments.

Then we had J. W. Dunne, also like Mottram, fascinated by transparency. In his case he painted the hooks white and used a kind of rayon floss called Cellulite for the body. The effect of this over a white hook created a certain impressive translucency but, as Jacques said, Dunne's flies went out of fashion because they were difficult to tie. Ultimately Cellulite was no longer produced. Dunne, however, is very readable (*Sunshine and the Dry Fly*, 1924,) and at times wrote brilliantly. Like this:

> The appeal of a sport - being simply an appeal to age-old inherited instincts - is never experienced in its full perfection unless there is involved some call upon that craft of the wilderness, that faculty of appreciating the ways of bird and beast, and fish and insect, the acquirement of which was, through countless centuries, the one great primary interest of primitive man.

Halford was now being attacked from all sides. In America Ernest Schwiebert denounced the Halford concept of precise imitation as preposterous. Another great American fisher, a follower of Harding, Vince Marinaro, said that even close imitation could not be defined.

> It cannot be done... in the way of Halford, Ronalds and others of ancient fame, for they spoke of imitation in terms of human vision and comprehension, supported only by the prop of entomology. That way alone lies grave error, since it does not take into account the vision of the trout and the geometry of the underwater world; and the study of entomology stops short, far short, of the approaches to these considerations, which are the dominant factors in devising imitations.
>
> (*A Modern Dry Fly Code*, 1950)

Marinaro moved his wings more towards the centre of the hook, tied the hackles in ways that supported the fly in the centre of balance and angled whisks like outriggers to the body. The humans thought it odd but the fish didn't.

The Scots invented the parachute dressing around the 1920s and it was taken up by the Canadians and then by the Americans and finally arrived on the Test as a parachute

Adams in the 1980s with the reputation of being almost, but not quite, infallible. Meanwhile the Amercians taught the English that there were times when flies that were too large were fished and produced proof with sizes 20 and smaller. Lee Wulff created his hair wings and Peter Deane his shadow mayflies, a dressing he had from J. Arthur Palethorpe of Newbury, Berkshire where they were first fished on the Kennet.

Shadow flies are entirely impressionist and have no body at all, only a grey palmered hackle and a couple of stubs of brown hackle for wings. They are, for some unaccountable reason, deadly during the big mayfly hatch.

In America again, Swisher and Richards produced flies without hackles which suggested they had gone back via Mottram to the Macedonians - but no, the flies had special arrangements of the wings and outrigger whisks.

In England - and again on the Kennet - Goddard and Clarke produced a remarkable book (*The Trout and the Fly*, 1980) which showed sequences of photographs of what flies and (horrifyingly) anglers looked like when seen by the trout, or rather the camera's eye, from underwater. Goddard's upside down flies did not sell well but his caddis became popular in the States.

And so we go on. Many flydressers are now experimenting with the use of new synthetic materials and the time will not be long, if it is not already here, when a fly will arrive which entirely consists of man-made materials from wings to tail.

Yet all these thoughts are still very advanced, for if you go along to the fishing tackle shops in London's Pall Mall you will not find all that number of new and experimental flies, but considerable numbers of the old-fashioned tyings of Greenwells, Pheasant Tails and Blue Duns.

In America and Canada, the most popular new salmon flies are known as buck bugs or just bugs and have names such as Green Machine. They are cigar shaped, without wings or hackle.

People have to be given time to get used to change, presumably due to the feeling, possibly the subconscious feeling, that what caught fish for their fathers will undoubtedly catch fish for their sons. They may also be right.

CHAPTER TWENTY

The Time of Our Lives

Pollution continues. Much of it is different but no less deadly. Especially deadly are the unseen pollutants, the so-called invisibles, the cumulative effects of acid rain and the leaching of the new agricultural chemicals, fertilisers and pesticides, into river systems and ground water. No one is quite certain what the effect will be on Britain's rivers by the 21st century.

A five year study (1985-1990) by scientists of the Royal Society in London together with scientists in Norway and Sweden reported that trout and salmon in up to a third of rivers and lakes in Scotland and in large areas of the Lake District, Wales and the Pennines have been wiped out or seriously affected by acid rain caused by fossil fuels, mainly the emissions from coal-burning power stations.

It was said that scientists were surprised at the extent of the damage, which must have been building up since 1850. Wind-blown acid rain is deposited on the land. This works on the aluminium in the soil which is leached out into rivers and deposited on the gills of fish who suffocate.

Studies of the upper waters of the Tweed in Scotland and the Tamar in south-west England have shown that large areas of the feeder streams are now so poisoned that they contain few, if any, fish. This may be due to acid rain or to the influx of farm chemicals and silage, deadly new pollutants of the last 30 or 40 years.

A report in *The Times* (2 February 1989) said there had been 'a tremendous increase in pollution' since 1976. A large part of the increase was caused by farm effluents. It was feared that some farm chemicals leaching into rivers could poison the spawning grounds not temporarily but for a number of years.

Figures in May 1990 from the Department of the Environment show that there were 12,600 reported cases of pollution in England and Wales in 1981, 23,257 in 1987, and 26,926 in 1988, the latest year for which figures were available. In other words, reported cases of pollution had more than doubled in seven years.

If this trend continues, and there is at present no indication that it will not, then by the time this book is published reported cases of pollution will be running at about 30,000 a year.

The two most significant causes of the increase in fish kill pollutants were the low quality of effluents from some sewage works and pollution from intensive agriculture and forestry (*Royal Commission on Environmental Pollution*, 1987).

It was reported that in north-west England one in five rivers was so contaminated that it could not support fish life. In May 1990, a Nature Conservancy ecologist, Dr Martin George, reported that something like 95 per cent of the Broads, the low-lying lakes in eastern England, had been killed by a blend of nitrate from farm fertilisers and phosphate from human sewage.

These chemicals create thick growths of slimey dark green algae which destroy healthy weeds and kill fish eggs and insect life unless swept away by floods. In the Broads there are insufficient floods. The water has become a dingy brown.

In southern England the chalksteams are suffering badly from water abstraction. At a conference of environmentalists at

Cambridge (*The Independent*, 1 October 1991) it was reported that some streams in south and south-east England had 'almost disappeared' because of water abstraction. Something like 70,000 licences to abstract water from rivers had been issued. These included borehole abstraction for public water supplies and abstraction by companies and individuals, either by pipe or borehole, amounting to many millions of gallons taken from the underground springs, the aquifers, that feed the chalkstreams.

At a time of drought (1990) the river Test was not only turbid from low flows (the visibility near Stockbridge was about six inches) but the river was noticeably lower. A water keeper on the upper Test was reported as saying that the level of the Test during the fishing season was now some ten to twelve inches below what it had been in the 1950s.

In September 1989, a National Rivers Authority was formed for England and Wales to be the 'guardian of the water environment' but it remains to be seen how effective a guardian it may become for its powers are limited compared with comparable organisations in the United States and Canada which operate under a different social structure.

At a time of world decline in Atlantic salmon catches, England, Wales, Ireland and Greenland are the only countries which still allow drift netting for salmon. Nets off the north-east coast of England take thousands of fish returning to Scottish rivers to spawn. The nets are to be phased out though it is not known when.

No one knows why the world catch has declined. Factory ships, over-killing, poaching, disease, a diminution in the supply of sea food, pollution from dumping nuclear waste - all these may be among the causes at sea. In addition there are the known and unknown effects of acid rain and pollution on river spawning grounds.

143

Plagues of sea lice have decimated seatrout stocks and in some cases annihilated the run in those areas of the west coasts of Scotland and Ireland where salmon farms have been established. There is also considerable anxiety about the long-term genetic effects of wild salmon spawning with farm salmon that have escaped from the sea cages. Storms wrecking cages allow thousands of salmon to escape.

All this is true, yet change is coming. We have already seen the first signs of it in the 1970s and 80s, a significant development of public concern to protect the environment, a sudden realisation and a subsequent alarm at the thought that we are poisoning our surroundings, the air and the land and the water in which we live and work and breathe.

Global warming, acid rain, nuclear and chemical disasters, have been the signs, the early warnings. the amber lights before the red, that have given us time to pause, to reassess, to think again.

Never before have so many government agencies and private organisations been set up in so short a time, a matter of a score of years, no more, to protect the environment from the many dangers that beset it. They have been working with a new sense of urgency not only to create cleaner air, land and water but to conserve those animals, fish and birds that inhabit these places who otherwise would be threatened with a slow extinction. We are no longer completely in the business of annihilating those creatures to whose future we have hitherto been almost entirely indifferent.

Killing no longer has quite the same attraction for us that it had. Big game is now as often as not pursued with a camera rather than a gun.

When in 1987 in a reservoir flyfishing competition in the English Midlands the winner killed 63 trout weighing more than 100 lbs, a trout fishing magazine came out strongly against

144

competition of this kind as 'it promotes too much slaughter'. When at about the same time, another magazine published a picture of some 50 salmon killed in a day, all laid out neatly on the river bank in front of the two smiling anglers who had caught them, protests poured in from readers who clearly had a sense of repugnance at the sight.

These are small incidents of their kind but one suspects they have a wider significance today than might have been anticipated at the time. Killing large numbers of fish is no longer a matter to provoke an uninhibited admiration, as it did in the days of our grandfathers or even those of our fathers.

The causes of this change are complex and involved. Perhaps our generation has seen too much killing, but it must be more than that. Perhaps we have become more sensitive to the pain of others. Perhaps we no longer think of what the Victorians called the 'brute creation' as being ours to treat with brutal indifference. Perhaps in preserving these lesser creatures we are subconsciously preserving ourselves.

It is an interesting speculation. What matters is that the killing and the over-killing is being restricted by various means and measures, some of them imposed and mandatory, some of them voluntary in order to preserve the stocks of wild fish, of the migratory salmon and seatrout and the natural trout of the rivers that otherwise might not survive.

Not that this is by any means a universal practice. There are some regions and some countries where nothing of this kind has yet taken place, where there are no limits on an angler's behaviour, where the rules of moderation set out so long ago by Berners still do not apply.

But change will come. The first signs of it are clear and strong and they will spread and grow. It is a historical process which would be exceptionally difficult or even impossible now to reverse, so that in spite of all the pollution and damage and dangers to our environment which appear at times as though they are about to overwhelm us, we have reasonable grounds for hope.

Appendix

The Roman Plume

There are many references in Homer and other Greek and Roman writers to fishing the plume for sea and estuary fish. The Romans made artificial wobblers from curved cow horn and used these as well as plumes for fishing with rod and line.

The main evidence for the use of the plume or the wobbler by the Romans during the occupation of Britain is in William Radcliffe's *Fishing from the Earliest Times* published by John Murray in 1921:

> Salmon appear but infrequently in representations, but plate 8, in C. W. King's *Roman Antiquities at Lydney Park, Gloucestershire*, London, 1879, shows in colour a mosaic dedicated to the god Nodons by Flavius Senilis, an officer in command of the fleet stationed off the Severn; this includes a number of *salmon*. King, ibid, plate 13, 2, is a diadem of beaten bronze representing a fisherman with a pointed cap in the act of hooking with undoubtedly a *tight* line a fine salmon: cf. A. B. Cook's discussion of these finds in *Folk-Lore*, 1906, XVI, 37ff. Nodons was in fact like Nuada, a fish god, indeed a Celtic understudy for Neptune. If salmon figure little in representations they bulk large in laws, and in commissariats for campaigns, e.g. 3000 dried salmon were ordered by Edward II in his war with Bruce.

The Treatyse

The best source for information about The *Treatyse of Fysshynge Wyth An Angle* (1496) is John McDonald's *The*

Origins of Angling published by Doubleday in New York in 1963. For one thing it contains the text of an earlier incomplete manuscript copy of the the *Treatyse* of about 1450 which is unique and is in the Yale University Library.

Copies of McDonald's book are not all that easy to obtain these days. I know of no copies that are available in England but a good second-hand bookseller in America might have one, such as Judith Bowman, Pound Ridge Road, Bedford, NY 10506. On the subject of the identity of Dame Juliana Berners, I am deeply indebted to research in the Westminster Abbey archives by Jack Heddon.

One of the virtues of the McDonald book is a translation of the Chaucerian English of the *Treatyse* into modern English. Reading the Berners advice on how fishermen should behave one has the feeling at times of reading a contemporary text book.

> I charge you that you break no man's hedges in going about your sports, nor open any man's gates without shutting them again. Also you must not use this aforesaid artful sport for covetousness, merely for the increasing and saving of your money, but mainly for your enjoyment and to procure the health of your body and more especially of your soul.

And what could be more modern than this later passage when you consider what happens these days on some of the salmon beats on Scottish rivers:

> Also you must not be too greedy in catching your game [the fish] as in taking too much at one time, a thing that could easily happen [for]...that could easily be the occasion of destroying your own sport and other men's also. When you have a sufficient mess [catch] you should covet no more at that time. Also you should busy yourself to nourish the game [the fishing]

148

in everything you can and to destroy all such things as are devourers of it.

It is good to repeat such advice as it brings the first English text book on fishing so much closer to our time. What is puzzling about Berners, however, is the brief, almost casual, description of the trout flies that are to be used throughout the season. As we said earlier detailed instructions are given on rod making but on flies - nothing at all!

There is a good deal of supposition about this. The most likely explanation is that the part of the manuscript from which the editor was working in the print shop in St Albans House which gave some instruction about fly tying was missing and that the editor of the manuscript, possibly Wynkyn de Worde himself, knowing nothing of the subject, made no effort to find out, probably taking the details that were given as sufficient. Here they are:

MARCH

The Dun Fly: The body of dun wool and the wings of the partridge.

Another Dun Fly: The body of black wool; the wings of the blackest drake; and the jay under the wing and under the tail.

APRIL

The Stone Fly: the body of black wool, and yellow under the wing and under the tail; and the wings, of the drake.

In the beginning of May, a good fly: the body of reddened wool and lapped about with black silk; the wings, of the drake and of the red capon's hackle.

MAY

The Yellow Fly: the body of yellow wool; the wings of the red cock's hackle and of the drake dyed yellow.

The Black Leaper: the body of black wool and lapped about with the herl of the peacock's tail; and the wings of the red capon with a blue head.

JUNE

The Dun Cut: the body of black wool and a yellow stripe along either side; the wings, of the buzzard, bound on with hemp that has been treated with tanbark.

The Maure Fly: the body of dusky wool; the wings of the blackest breast feathers of the wild drake.

The Tandy Fly: at St William's Day: the body of tandy wool; and the wings the opposite, either against the other, of the whitest breast feathers of the wild drake.

JULY

The Wasp Fly: the body of black wool and lapped about with yellow thread; the wings, of the buzzard.

The Shell Fly at St Thomas's Day: the body of green wool and lapped about with the herl of the peacock's tail; wings, of the buzzard.

AUGUST

The Drake Fly: the body of black wool and lapped about with black silk; wings of the breast feathers of the black drake with a black head.

McDonald took the trouble to check what Waller Hills and G.E.M. Skues, two good flydressers, thought of the Berners dressings, and whether they could identify them. They agreed on three: the second Dun Fly was an olive, and the Stone Fly was indeed a stone fly, and the Black Leaper was a caddis. Then, they disagreed.

Skues thought the first Dun Fly was a March Brown while Hills thought it was a February Red. The Ruddy Fly was either a Red Spinner or a Great Red Spinner. They were doubtful about the Yellow Fly which might or might not have been the Little Yellow May Dun. The Dun Cut was either a Yellow Dun or a Caddis, the Maure Fly a Green Drake or an Alder, the Tandy a Grey Drake or an Oak Fly, the Wasp Fly was a wasp or a crane fly, the Shell Fly a grannom or a caddis, and the Drake Fly Hills thought was an alder.

The Venables Text

The following is the full quotation of the summary given on page 22:

> In general, all sorts of flies are very good in their season, for such fish as will rise at the fly, viz. Salmon, Trout, Umber, Grayling, Bleak, Chevin, Roach, Dace, etc. Though some of these fish do love some flies better than others, except the fish named, I know not any sort or kind that will ordinarily and freely rise at the fly, though I know some who will angle for Bream and pike with artificial flies, though I judge this labour lost, and the knowledge a needless curiosity; those fish being taken much easier, especially the Pike, by other ways.
>
> All the aforementioned sorts of fish will sometimes take the fly much better at the top of the water, and at another time much

151

better a little under the superficies of the water; and in this your own observation must be your constant and daily instructor; for if they will not rise to the top try them under, it being impossible, in my opinion, to give any certain rule in this particular; also the five sorts of fish first named will take the artificial fly, so will not the other, except an oak worm or cad-bait be put on the point of the hook, or some other worm suitable, as the fly must be, to the season.

Charles Cotton's Flies

Charles Cotton (1630-1687) translator, poet, country squire, fisherman and friend of Izaak Walton who contributed the second part of Walton's *Compleat Angler*, is notable for having produced some 63 dressings of trout flies. It is doubtful whether they are all his own dressings. Most probably a number of them were traditional Derbyshire flies for the River Dove. Derivations of some of them are in use today.

Many of Cotton's flies are difficult to relate to the natural insect. One finds it impossible to make sense of dressings like the Violet Fly which is made 'of dark violet stuff with the wings of the grey feather of a mallard.'

After a fly called a Thorn Tree Fly which is said to have had a great repute, he goes on:

There is beside this another BLUE DUN: the dubbing of which is made thus to be got. Take a small toothcomb, and with it comb the neck of a black greyhound, and the down that sticks in the teeth will be the finest blue that you ever saw. The wings of this fly can hardly be too white; and he is taken about the tenth of this month [March] and lasteth till the four and twentieth. From the tenth of this month also, till towards the end, is taken a little BLACK GNAT. The dubbing either of the fur of a black water-dog

152

or the down of a young black water-coot; the wings of the male of the Mallard as white as may be; the body as little as you can possibly make it, and the wings as short as his body.

The trouble about Cotton is that one never quite knows which natural fly he is dealing with - his Great Hackle is presumably a mayfly but one cannot be absolutely certain - and there are additional problems about his use of somewhat esoteric materials. How many flydressers would normally have access to an amenable black greyhound?

The time of Charles Cotton and Robert Venables is notable not only for the large number of text books that were produced on flyfishing but also of course for that great angling classic, Izaak Walton's *Compleat Angler*. As a matter of interest, the following were the authors of flyfishing books and books on fish and insect life published from the late 16th to the end of the 17th century:

Samuel, 1572. Mascall, 1599. Taverner, 1600. Dennys, 1606. Markham, 1614. Lawson, c 1617. Barker, 1651. Walton, 1653. Venables, 1662. Franck, 1674. Cotton, 1676. Chetham, 1681. Smith, 1696.

Scotcher of Chepstow

Jack Heddon in the introduction to the Honeydun edition of Scotcher's *Fly Fisher's Legacy* noted that

It was the first angling book devoted entirely to flyfishing and certainly the first to mention the use of stiffer rods and steeply tapered lines that will enable you to throw with exactness against the wind when necessary.

Heddon and his partner John Simpson were able to date the book about 1810 after research in the British Museum. They have also suggested that Scotcher was a pen name used by a local doctor, Mark Willet of 33 Moor Street, Chepstow, who was also the local printer. Heddon points out that Scotcher, Salter, Bowlker and Lascelles *(Angling,* 1811,) were all

> upstream anglers who fished with an imitation of the insect that was hatching or on the water. They had a common bond in Wales and the west of England. Wales must have been to the 18th century angler what Hampshire became to anglers at the end of the 19th century.

None were as rigid about upstream fishing as their descendants in Hampshire. Scotcher advocates fishing the food stream when there were no rises and made it quite clear that there were times when the sunk fly was best.

> In windy weather and low water fish rise mostly at the slow end of small streams or on the long flats of deep water, if not too deep; you may then let your fly be just under the surface... Be very cautious in approaching the water for if you are once seen all chance of success is over. Sometimes throw up a stream, sometimes down, as you can be best concealed.

He tied flies on quite small hooks, a Black Gnat on the equivalent of our Redditch scale 16 hook with a very small blob of peacock herl for the body and a very light blue dun hen hackle. His Hawthorn Fly is very modern: a body of black ostrich herl, light starling wings and two turns of a long-fibred black hackle for the legs.

What is of interest is that though Scotcher - or Dr Willet - advises his readers to fish the fly floating or sunk as the case may be he does not say how one is to keep the fly 'aloft on top of the water' or for that matter to sink it.

He never makes any mention of drying the fly by whisking it through the air to make it float. One can only come to the

154

conclusion that the tactic of drying the fly was so obvious to his contemporaries it did not need to be mentioned, as indeed was the case with Bowlker and other writers. Even so one would have thought that a text book on fishing the fly might not have neglected such an important factor of presentation.

Alfred Ronalds

Ronalds was a remarkable man. Having felt the inadequacy of mere verbal instruction to enable him to imitate the natural fly correctly, or even approximately, and the little utility of graphical illustrations unaccompanied by the principal requisite - colour - he has been induced to paint both the natural and the artificial fly from nature, to etch them with his own hand, and to colour or to superintend the colouring of each particular impression.

So wrote 'Piscator', whoever he was, perhaps Ronalds himself, in the preface to the *Fly Fisher's Entomology*, first published in 1836. It was 'an entirely original work and so magnificently illustrated that the coloured copperplates remain unsurpassed to this day. At once the standard of illustration was raised and the new school of angler-naturalist was founded at last' (W. H. Lawrie).

An example of the Ronalds illustrations is on Plate 7. Details are given in his text of 46 natural flies and their matching artificials together with their scientific classification. In each case he describes what the natural fly looks like, followed by the dressing of the imitation.

These four examples give an idea of the detailed work that was involved:

THE BLUE DUN

This fly lives three or four days in the state represented; then becomes the Red Spinner. It begins to be plentiful in the early part of March, should the weather be mild. When in full season it will be found on the water chiefly on rather cold windy days. It endeavours to take flight three or four seconds after emerging from the Pupa. On cold days it seems to have rather more difficulty in rising from the water than in warm weather, and consequently becomes very frequently food for fishes at the moment of its assuming the winged state.

Imitation

Body: Fur of a hare's ear or face, spun very thinly on fine yellow silk and wound on thickest at the shoulder. Some of the dubbing is then picked out to form legs.

Tail: Two fibres of a Dun Hackle.

Wings: From a quill feather of a starling's wing which may be slightly stained in onion dye.

Legs: If a sufficient quantity of dubbing cannot be picked out for the legs two or three turns of a Ginger Dun hackle can be added and will help to keep the wings upright. Put these on last, whipping them on the bare hook and finish at the head. Hook No 2, Grayling.

Remarks: This elegant fly kills well till June made as follows: Body of yellow silk waxed with a very little Blue Dun fur from rat, mouse, mole or rabbit spun upon the silk so that the yellow shows through. Body tapering from shoulder to tail. Legs: A Honey Dun hackle, four or five turns. Wings: A starling's quill

156

feather put on last on the bare hook so as to stand up boldly. Thus made it is a good fly for parr. When you can put this fly together well you have reason to hope you are improving: for the Duns are delicate insects to imitate. Wax your silk lightly.

THE GREEN DRAKE, MAY FLY, CADOW

This fly, proceeding from a water nympha, lives three or four days as shown, then the female changes to the Grey Drake and the male to the Black Drake. The Green Drake cannot be said to be in season quite three weeks on average. Its season depends greatly on the state of the weather; and it will be found earlier on the slowly running parts of the stream (such as mill dams) than on the rapid places.

Imitation

Body: The middle part is of pale straw-coloured floss silk, ribbed with silver twist. The extremities are of a brown peacock's herl, tied with light brown silk thread. Tail: Three rabbit's whiskers.

Wings and Legs: Made buzz from a mottled feather of the mallard stained a pale greenish yellow. Hook No 5, 6 or 7 long.

To make it with wings in their state of rest part of a feather similarly stained must be used, and a pale brown bittern's hackle, or in case of need a partridge feather must be wrapped round the same body under the wings.

THE CINNAMON FLY

This fly comes from a water pupa. There are many species. The larger ones being stronger can resist the force of rain and wind better than that represented and are therefore not so well known to the fish. It should be used after a heavy shower and also on a windy day. In both cases very great diversion may be expected with it.

Imitation

Body: Fawn coloured floss silk, tied on with silk thread of the same colour.

Wings: Feather of a yellow-brown hen's wing, rather darker than the landrail's wing feather.

Legs: A ginger hackle. It is made buzz with a red hackle from the grouse, or a red hackle stained brown with copperas and tied on the same body. Hook No 3, long.

Remarks: So numerous are the species of Caddis Fly resembling the above, different on different waters, that the angler must use his own observation. A wren's tail feather wound round a hare's ear body will aid him in giving the rich brown tint common to many of the genus, and the landrail's quill feather will be sufficiently dark with this hackle.

GOLDEN DUN MIDGE

The male has feathered antennae which the female has not. It seems to require a warm day to disengage itself from its water nympha. On such days very great sport may be had with it until the end of May. In its larva state it is the Blood-worm of anglers.

Imitation

Body: Olive floss silk ribbed with gold twist, and tied with dun silk thread.

Wings: From the palest feather of a young starling.

Legs: A pure dun hackle wound on in front of the wings. Hook No 1, Grayling.

Remarks: No fly is more abundant, especially in showery weather and just after rain. It is a prime favourite on the Dove. A delicate hand is required to make this fly *handsomely* and the finest silk. Though shoemaker's soft wax is generally to be preferred, as most durable, colourless wax has an advantage for making delicate flies like this and the Jenny Spinner.

Ronalds' instructions have little or no indication how his artificials should be presented. He gives the impression that he fished downstream except in the case of what he calls brooks - presumably quite small streams - where the upstream fly or worm could be used. His Blue Dun is clearly more of a wet fly than a dry. His dressings were fairly soon outdated by the work of Foster, Hall, Marryat, Halford and others. However, he was the first fisherman-entomologist to show the natural flies in colour and to define the various species to which they belonged.

George Pulman and the Dry Fly

G. P. R. Pulman had a newsagent's and fishing tackle shop at Axminster with branches at Dorchester and Totnes and fished the Axe for most of his life. His *Vade Mecum of Fly Fishing for Trout* in 1841 contained the first use of the word 'dry fly', meaning a fly freshly taken from wallet or box which would float better because it was dry than one already soaked. This is the relevant passage:

So, as it is not in the nature of things that this soaked artificial fly can swim upon the surface like the natural ones do, it follows the alternative and sinks below the rising fish, the notice of which it entirely escapes, because they happen to be looking upwards for the materials of their meal.

Let a dry fly be substituted for a wet one, the line switched a few times through the air to throw off the superabundant moisture, a judicious cast made just above the rising fish, and the fly allowed to float towards and over them, and the chances are ten to one it will be seized as readily as the living insect.

This dry fly, we must remark, must be an imitation of the natural fly on which the fish are feeding because if widely different the fish instead of being allured would most likely be surprised and startled at the novelty presented and would suspend feeding until the appearance of their favourite and familiar prey.

We mention this as an illustration of the importance of imitating action, and must not be understood to recommend the constantly substituting of a dry fly for a wet one over every rising fish. Better, as a general rule, when the angler after a few casts finds the fish over which he throws unwilling to be tempted, to pass on in search of a more willing victim.

See also page 166.

The Upstream Wet Fly

The term 'wet fly' in upstream fishing according to the North of England and Border styles needs modifying a little. A team of wet flies or just a single wet fly is fished upstream with short drifts and in many cases the flies are taken while they are still on the surface on the drift before they have had a chance to sink.

In practice, the flies are fished both wet and dry on a drift, the dry fly often being that of the bob which sometimes rides the water, sometimes skims over it and daps. Those protagonists of upstream fishing such as Stewart on the Borders (Chapter 6, page 53) would have been most surprised that anyone should bother to discriminate between wet and dry when their flies were sometimes on the surface and sometimes just below on the same cast.

The patterns for the fast flowing and often rocky streams of the Borders and the North of England are known to date from the 18th century and one can reasonably assume that they go way back beyond that. They have no connection with the Berners patterns which were probably unknown to northern flydressers.

Pritt and other northerners have given details of the Yorkshire flies which, like the Border patterns, suggest duns tumbled in the fast water, spinners or possibly stoneflies and caddis. They are intended to create the illusion of flies rather than imitations. The long fine hackles add to that impression.

Two Yorkshiremen, Harfield Edmonds and Norman Lee, in *Brook and River Trouting*, privately published in Bradford in 1916, give coloured illustrations of upstream patterns and details of the dressings on hook sizes 14 and 16 Redditch scale.

They are probably much the same flies as those fished a hundred or two hundred years earlier. These are some of the best known:

ORANGE PARTRIDGE

Perlidae and Ephermeridae

Wings: Hackled with a brown mottled (not barred) feather from a Partridge's neck or back.

Body: Orange silk by itself or ribbed with about four turns of gold wire or tinsel.

Head: Orange silk.

March to middle of May.

DARK SNIPE OR SNIPE AND PURPLE

Ephemeridae

Wings: Hackled with the dark feather from the marginal coverts of a Snipe's wing.

Body: Purple silk.

Head: Purple silk.

March to middle of April and again in September.

DARK WATCHET OR IRON BLUE DUN

Ephemeridae

Wings: Hackled with a dark smokey blue feather from a Jackdaw's throat.

Body: Orange and purple silk, twisted together, dubbed very sparingly with Mole's fur and wound on the body so that the orange and purple show in alternate bands.

Head: Orange Silk.

Last week in April and throughout May and sometimes early June. Particularly for dull days.

BLACK GNAT

Diptera

Wings: A few fibres from a light blue hen's hackle put on as a single wing.

Body: Black silk.

Legs: Rusty black Hen Hackle.

Head: Black silk.

Kelson's Salmon Flies

George M. Kelson, one of flyfishing's great egoists, published his remarkable book, *The Salmon Fly*, privately, in 1895. It set out how the choice of fly on any particular day could be made on 'well-ascertained principles' though it was never quite clear what these were. He developed 'special standard dressings' for taking salmon in various rivers and in particular places.

Rivers he classified by colour as being blue, red, yellow or grey, though the basis for such classification remained obscure. This is one of his 'specials', Elsie, which was designed 'for taking fish lying behind upright rocks and large boulders'.

ELSIE

Tag: Silver twist (plenty).

Tail: A topping and Summer Duck.

Butt: Black herl.

Body: One third light blue silk, ribbed with silver twist and butted with fibres of Grande Breve Tocate above and below, and black herl; followed by claret silk having a dark claret hackle along it and ribbed with silver tinsel (oval).

Wings: Tippet fibres (plenty) veiled with Mallard; and a topping.

Throat: Jay.

Sides: Jungle (extra size) and a short strip of large Summer Duck.

Cheeks: Grand Breve Tocate (extra size).

Efforts have been made to identify Grand Breve Tocate without success.

Another of his 'specials' was the Variegated Sun Fly which he said was 'the only fly which would take fish in bright sunshine' and was very cross if anyone doubted his word. This particular fly, he said, was intended for what he called 'blue rivers' such as the Tweed.

THE VARIEGATED SUN FLY

Tag: Silver Twist.

Tail: A topping and powder blue Macaw.

Body: In coils, wasp fashion and spindle shaped, of red, black, yellow and blue Berlin wool.

Throat: Black hackle.

Wings: Six toppings.

Horns: Blue Macaw.

Fortunately, Kelson, whatever his conceit, left us some superb examples of Victorian flydressing such as the Jock Scott. This was created by John Scott (1817-1893) of Branxholm who worked as a ghillie for several Scottish lairds. This is Kelson's version of the original which probably follows it fairly closely:

JOCK SCOTT

Tag: Silver twist and yellow silk.

Tail: A topping and India crow.

Butt: Black herl.

Body: In two equal sections: No. 1 of yellow silk (buttercup colour) ribbed with narrow silver tinsel and butted with Toucan above and below, and black herl. No. 2 black silk ribbed with broad silver tinsel.

Hackle: A natural black hackle.

Throat: Gallina.

Wings: Two strips of black Turkey with white tips, Golden Pheasant tail, Bustard, grey Mallard, Peacock sword feather, swan dyed blue and yellow, Red Macaw, Mallard and a topping.

Sides: Jungle.

Cheeks: Chatterer.Horns: Blue Macaw.

Head: Black herl.

The Dry Fly and the Floating Fly

A good deal of confusion exists about dry flies and floating flies. The original artificial flies of the Macedonians and those given by Berners were imitations of winged insects, flying insects, which are normally found in the air or on the surface of the water. If fished with a horsehair line these imitation flies can be made to float. They can also be dapped on the surface and sink a little below the surface when they would become what we now call emergers. The intention was to put the artificial fly where the real flies were being eaten by the trout. These flies were either hatching, floating or ovipositing, and the intention of the early anglers was to make their artificial flies behave in the same way. With primitive patterns it was not all that easy but as we now know it can be done.

The first precise description how the artificial fly should be fished on top of the water was possibly that given by William Shipley who kept a fishing diary from about 1780 onwards. He describes how to use the false cast to dry the fly:

> Let your flies float gently down the water, working them gradually towards you, making a fresh cast every two or three yards you fish. We do strictly recommend frequent casts for ... the quick repetition of casting keeps them lighter and drier than if they were left to float a longer time on the water.

There are many other examples, mostly following on from

166

Shipley, including Scotcher, Martin, Sir Humphrey Davy and others, like Thad Norris in the United States. But what seems to be the best description of the dry fly technique was first given in the mid 1800s by David Foster of Ashbourne in Derbyshire.

Foster (1815-c1875) fished the same river as Charles Cotton, the Derbyshire Dove, and kept a fishing diary which was published, posthumously, by his sons as *The Scientific Angler* in 1882. His description of dry flyfishing probably dates from the mid-1800s:

> It is Foster's presentation that matters most. A discussion why legs in the floating fly should be ample and full to promote flotation... it is all there, false casting to dry the flies, making sure the wings on the dry fly cock properly as they float along, the virtue of fishing both up and down stream, the avoidance of drag...it is impressively complete. (Paul Schullery)

So far as I can tell, the only difference between Foster's flies and the split-wing floaters that were to come some 30 years later is in the winging. Foster used a quill feather doubled to make his upright wings but that is really a minor point. The hackle for the legs, ample and full to assist floatation, was tied on after the wings. Like Halford, he fished the dry fly both upstream and down as the need arose, but mostly up, and he goes on:

> The wings of the duns must be full and erect, or cock-up as it is sometimes designated, so as to admit the fly to be comparatively dry for some little time when, becoming saturated, a few backwards and forwards whisks of the line and rod should be given before the delivery of the cast again. This is repeated whenever the flies become saturated as by so doing the trouble of repeatedly changing the lure is greatly lessened.

He urged that the dry fly should be fished on the Dove and on similar waters as it was:

> by far the most scientific and artistic way of alluring trout or grayling, and well-fished streams will yield more and heavier dishes of fish to it than any other method or system of angling whatever.

His fly dressings were good but the book as a whole received less attention than it deserved because on the date of publication (1882) there was already a good deal of advanced publicity about the split-wing floaters on the Hampshire chalkstreams.

Foster had two dressings for the big mayfly (Ephemera danica, or the Green Drake) and this is one:

Body: Straw coloured mohair

Rib: Gold twist

Wings: Mallard slightly dyed yellow

Legs: Honey dun cock's hackle

Head: Peacock herl or copper-coloured silk

One problem with Foster's dressings which may have put off some of his contemporaries was that he matched his flies by what he called their shades. For example his Blue Dun had a shade for February as well as a similar shade for November. This was the autumn shade:

Body: Blue fur spun on yellow silk

Wings: Fieldfare

Legs: Light dun hackle

His Olive or April Dun could also be used in September because the shade of the fly was similar for both. Here is his Olive Dun which is pretty close to some of our contemporary patterns:

Body: Blue fur spun on yellow silk

Wing: Pale starling

Legs: Light dun hackle freckled or stained yellow

This is an interesting definition of a dry fly by Vincent Marinaro in *The Ring of the Rise* (1976):

> We must begin with the proposition that no matter how dry the fly is, it must touch the water and be exposed to the air at the same time. If this idea is carried out to its logical conclusion all of us must agree that if the smallest portion is exposed to the air no matter how deeply submerged the fly may be, it is still a legitimate form of the dry fly.

Marinaro's definition seems to link up nicely with the story of Horace Brown, a former president of the Piscatorial Society, who was asked whether all the trout he had caught on a particular day were taken on the dry fly to which he replied that the thought some of them might have been slightly damp.

Most of the information about that great dry fly man, Frederic M. Halford have been given in the main text on pages 91 to 98.

For those who would like to know more, the Centenary Edition of *Dry Fly Fishing in Theory and Practice*, with a preface by Dermot Wilson, was published in 1989 by H. F. & G. Witherby of 14 Henrietta Street, London WC2E 8QJ. The original editions of Halford's books are rarely on the market and are expensive. John and Judith Head of Crane Street, Salisbury, Wiltshire sometimes have copies. A rare deluxe edition of *Dry Fly Entomology* is listed in an Amercian catalogue (Judith Bowman Books, Pound Ridge Road, Bedford, NY 10506) at $1,000.

G. E. M. Skues

Without any question, Skues is the most readable of all the Victorian-Edwardian writers. One ploughs through Halford almost as a matter of duty. One turns to any one of Skues' books with relief. It is true that Skues' nymph patterns are rarely seen these days. They have been overshadowed by Sawyer's simplistic weighted pattern.

A complete list of the Skues nymphs together with an account of the great debate in the Flyfishers' Club on the morality of nymph fishing is in *The Way of a Man with a Trout* by Donald Overfield. I have taken three patterns of Skues' nymphs which are well worth trying on the chalkstreams:

IRON BLUE NYMPH

Hook: 00, dressed to gut [16 Redditch scale].

Body: Crimson tying silk dubbed with mole's fur.

Whisks: Soft white cock saddle hackle fibres from near the root of the feather.

Hackle: Shortest blue-black feather from the throat of an old jackdaw.

170

PALE WATERY NYMPH

Hook: 00, [16 Redditch scale].

Silk: Primrose.

Hackle: Dark blue hen or henny cock, very short and not more than two turns.

Whisks: To match the hackle. Very short.

Dubbing: Blue squirrels fur.

Rib: Yellow silk.

MEDIUM OLIVE NYMPH

Hook: No. 15, down-eyed Pennell sneck or No. 1 Pryce Tannatt's round bend.

Silk: Primrose waxed with clear wax.

Hackle: Short woolly blue feather from the breast of a blue bantam hen. Three turns.

Whisks: Three strands of woolly feather from the breast of a cock tied in short.

Rib: Yellow silk, gold wire, or none.

Body: Hare's ear or for lighter pattern hare's poll [head].

Skues' books are:
Minor Tactics of the Chalkstream (1910); *The Way of a Trout with a Fly* (1921); *Sidelines, Sidelights and Reflections* (1932);

Nymph Fishing for Chalkstream Trout (1939) and post-humously *Itchen Memories* (1951). His angling letters edited by C. F. Walker were published in 1956.

H. S. Hall and the Dry Fly

In *Sidelines, Sidelights and Reflections* (1932) G. E. M. Skues gives his reasons why he believes H. S. Hall evolved the modern floating fly, the split-wing floater. He wrote:

Floating Flies and How to Dress Them was published by Halford in 1886 and it was on April 28th, 1879, that Halford and Marryat first met in old John Hammonds' shop near the Square in Winchester, and according to Halford's *Autobiography* it was before the end of 1880 that the decision to write *Floating Flies* was taken. It will be remembered that the book insists firmly (and quite rightly) on the necessity of using slips from corresponding feathers in opposite wings of the same bird, and that the materials for the volume were worked out by the author in concert with Marryat. Moreover I recall specimens of floating flies so dressed by Mrs Cox (then of Winchester) and Mrs Brocas shown at the Fisheries Exhibition in 1883. So I infer that the patterns in Marryat's book which are dressed otherwise certainly antedate 1886 and probably 1883. A great many shop-tied patterns continued to be tied in the old manner for many years after but few of the examples in Marryat's fly book are 'Shop'uns'.

A letter of H. S. Hall in *The Field* of August 5, 1882, describes elaborately the tying of upwinged double-dressed floaters on eyed hooks - and , though he there recommends the use of the same feather for both pairs of wings, he does say that 'anyone who considers excessive neatness the first consideration will

172

have to pick his two wings separately from right and left feathers.' So, though he then preferred the older methods, he was fully aware that a neater fly could be produced by slips from corresponding feathers in opposite wings.

It has not indeed been generally realised and for my part I confess I had not realised that the present day and the preceding generation owe to H. S. Hall the evolution of the modern floating fly as well as the eyed hook, universally known by his name. The facts I have now elicited seem to place him in front of both Marryat and Halford as the father of the modern split-wing floater.

Dr H. A. Bell

Dr Bell's original patterns of flies for reservoir fishing were copied by Donald Carr or Lawrie Williamson, the Blagdon bailiffs, during the time that Bell was fishing there. They were simpler patterns than those which were tied later by commercial dressers. These are three:

THE GRENADIER

Body: Scarlet wool, the colour of a Grenadier's dress uniform.

Rib: Fine silver tinsel.

Hackle: A fine couple of turns of dun-coloured hackle.

THE BLAGDON BUZZER

Body: Black wool, thin at the base and thicker at the head of the fly, secured by fine silver wire.

THE AMBER NYMPH

Body: Amber coloured wool, rather cigar shaped, ribbed by fine silver tinsel.

Hackle: A couple of turns of light-coloured dun hackle sloping well back.

Bell may also have tied the Green Midge, mentioned by Sheridan as far back as 1907 as creating a very heavy rise to the winged fly but the standard pattern, probably that from Carr or Williamson, is one that can be fished on the surface or just below. The body is of emerald green wool with a stiff white hackle at the shoulder.

Bibliography

There are many good fishing entomologists on both sides of the Atlantic these days but the one that has had the most influence in Britain is John Goddard who has taken on the mantle of a modern Ronalds. No small history would be complete without mentioning his two major works, *Trout Fly Recognition* (1966) and *Trout Flies of Stillwater* (1969).

Goddard was born in London in 1923 and began fishing as a schoolboy. He was a paratrooper in World War II and afterwards, as head of the family fishing tackle firm, E. F. Goddard and Co, he became interested and then absorbed in the study of flies and their matching artificials. He is still doing research on the water he fishes, which is the Wilderness beat of the Kennet.

I owe a great deal to Goddard's two books and also to the authors of the following books, articles and catalogues from which I have quoted or which have provided valuable information:

Ashley-Cooper, John. *A Salmon Fisher's Odyssey*, Witherby, 1982. *A Line on Salmon*, Witherby, 1983.

Bainbridge, George. *The Fly Fisher's Guide*, 1816.

Barker, Thomas. *The Art of Angling*, 1659.

Bates, J. D. *The Art of the Atlantic Salmon Fly*, Swan Hill Press, 1990.

Baily's Magazine. Halford article, December 1899.

Behrendt, Alex. *The Management of Angling Waters*, Andre Deutsch, 1977.

Best, George. *The Art of Angling*, 1814.

Blacker, William. *The Art of Angling*, 1842.

Bridgett R. C. *Loch Fishing in Theory and Practice*, 1924.

Bridges, Anthony. *Modern Salmon Fishing*, Black, 1939.

Brookes, J. *The Art of Angling*, 1740.

Buckland, John, and Oglesby, Arthur. *A Guide to Salmon Flies*, Crowood, 1990.

Bucknall, Geoffrey. *Fly Fishing Tactics on Stillwater*, Muller, 1966.

Church, Bob. *Reservoir Trout Fishing*, Black, 1983.

Chrystal, Major R, A. *Angling at Lochboisdale*, Witherby, 1939.

Clarke, Brian. *The Pursuit of Stillwater Trout*, Black, 1975.

Cutcliffe, H. C. *The Art of Trout Fishing in Rapid Streams*, 1863 and the Sampson Low edition of 1883.

Davy, Sir Humphrey. *Salmonia,* Murray, 1828.

Dunne, J. W. *Sunshine and the Dry Fly*, Black, 1924.

Edmonds and Lee, *Brook and River Trouting*, 1916 and the

Orange Partridge Press edition, 1980.

Falkus, Hugh. *Salmon Fishing*, Witherby, 1984.

Francis, Austin M. *Catskill Rivers*, Nick Lyons Books, 1983.

Foster, David. *The Scientific Angler*, 1882.

Franck, Richard. *Northern Memoirs*, 1658, Constable, 1821.

Frost, Dr Winifred E. *A Survey of the Rainbow Trout in Britain and Ireland*, Salmon and Trout Association, no.date., probably 1973.

Greene, Harry Plunket. *Where the Bright Waters Meet*, Allen, 1929 and Witherby, 1964.

Gingrich, Arnold. *The Fishing in Print,* Winchester Press, New York, 1974.

Grey, Sir Edward. *Fly Fishing*, 1899, Dent, 1930.

Halford, Frederic M. *Dry Fly Fishing in Theory and Practice*, 1889. Centenary edition Witherby, 1989. *Floating Flies and How to Dress Them*, London, Low, 1886. *Dry Fly Entomology*, London, Vinton, 1897.

Hardy's Anglers Guide, no date, c 1930 and 1952.

Harding, Colonel E. W. *The FlyFisher and the Trout's Point of View*, Seeley, 1931.

Harmsworth's Encyclopedia, no date, c 1910.

Harris, J. R. *An Angler's Entomology*, Collins, 1952.

Heddon, Jack. Article on the dry fly, *Encyclopedia of Fly Fishing*, Batsford, 1986.

Hewitt, E. R. *Secrets of the Salmon*, Scribners, New York, 1922.

Hills, J. Waller. *A History of Fishing for Trout*, Stokes, 1921.

Hopkins, Harry. *The Long Affray*, Secker, 1968.

Heywood, Gerald. *Charles Cotton and His River*, Sherrat and Hughes, Manchester, 1928.

Jacques, David. *Fisherman's Fly*, Black, 1965. *The Development of Modern Stillwater Fishing*, Black, 1974.

Kelson, George M. *The Salmon Fly*, privately printed, 1895.

Kingsmill Moore, T. C. *A Man May Fish*, Jenkins, 1960.

Kite, Oliver. *A Fisherman's Diary*, Deutsch, 1969.

Kirkbride. *The Northern Angler*, 1837.

Klein, Louis. *River Pollution*, vol 3, Butterworth, 1966.

Lane, Joscelyn. *Lake and Loch Fishing*, Seeley, 1954.

Lapsley, Peter. *Trout From Stillwaters*, Black, 1982, Unwin Hyman, 1988.

Lawrie, W. H. *A Reference Book of English Trout Flies*, Pelham, 1967.

Love, Harold (ed.). Charles Cotton's poems in *The Penguin Book of Restoration Verse*, 1968.

Lunn, Mick, with Graham-Ranger, Clive. *A Particular Lunn*, Unwin Hyman, 1990.

Lyons, Nick. *Bright Rivers*, Lippincott, New York, 1977.

Malone, E. J. *Irish Trout and Salmon Flies.* Colin Smythe,1981

Marshall, Howard. *Reflections on a River*, Witherby, 1967.

Martin, James. *The Anglers Guide*, 1854.

Martin, Alexander. Fishing Tackle Catalogue, Glasgow, c.1920-30.

Mottram, J. C. *Fly Fishing: Some new Arts and Mysteries*, The Field, no date, possibly 1915.

Marinaro, Vincent. *In the Ring of the Rise*, 1976.

McCaskie, H. B. *The Guileless Trout*, Cresset, 1950.

McDonald, John. *The Origins of Angling*, Doubleday, New York, 1963.

Macintosh, Alexander. *The Driffield Angler*, 1808.

McLaren, Charles. *Fishing for Salmon*, Donald, Edinburgh, 1977, Unwin Hyman 1988.

Netboy, A. *The Atlantic Salmon*, Faber, 1968.

Newland, Henry. *The Erne, its Legends and its Flyfishing*, 1851

Overfield, T. Donald. *G. E. M. Skues: The Way of a Man with a Trout*, Benn, 1977. *Famous Flies and Their Originators*, Black, 1972.

Phillips, Ernest. *Trout in Lakes and Reservoirs.* Longmans, 1914.

Pulman, G. P. R. *The Vade Mecum of Fly Fishing for Trout*, 1841.

Pool, J. Lawrence and Angeline J. Pool. *Walton: The Compleat Angler and His Turbulent Times*, Stineham Press, New York, 1976.

Radcliffe, William. *Fishing From the Earliest Times*, Murray, 1921.

Ransome, Arthur. *Rod and Line*, Cape, 1929, OUP, 1980.

Ronalds, Alfred. *The Fly Fisher's Entomology*, Longmans, 1836, 6th edition 1862.

Scotcher, George. *The Fly Fisher's Legacy*, 1800, Honeydun Press, 1974.

Sawyer, Frank. *Nymphs and the Trout*, Black, 1958.

Schullery, Paul. *American Fly Fishing: A History*, Nick Lyons Books, New York, 1987.

Scrope, William. *Days and Nights of Salmon Fishing on the Tweed*, 1843.

Shipley, William. *A True Treatise of the Art of Fly Fishing, Trolling, etc*, 1838.

Skues, G. E. M. *Minor Tactics of the Chalk Stream*, Black, 1910. *The Way of a Trout with a Fly*, Black, 1921. *Sidelines, Sidelights and Reflections*, Seeley, 1932.

Stewart, W. C. *The Practical Angler*, 1857, 1919.

Taverner, John. *Certaine Experiments Concerning Fish and Fruits*, 1600.

Taverner, Eric. *Divers Ways to Tackle Trout*, Chatto, 1925. *Trout Fishing from All Angles*, Seeley, 1929.

BIBLIOGRAPHY

Traver, Robert. *Anatomy of a Fisherman*, Nick Lyons Books, New York.

Trevelyan, G. M. *English Social History*, Longman, 1942.

Venables, Colonel Robert. *The Experienced Angler*, 1662. Antrobus Press edition, 1969.

Voss Bark, Anne (ed.) *West Country Fly Fishing*, Batsford, 1983.

Voss Bark, Conrad. *The Encyclopedia of Fly Fishing*, Batsford, 1983.

Walker, C. F. *Lake Flies and Their Imitation*, Jenkins, 1960.

Walker, Richard. *Dick Walker's Trout Fishing*, David and Charles, 1982.

Walton, Izaak and Cotton, Charles. *The Compleat Angler*, mainly the Folio Society edition, 1949.

Wanless, Alexander. *Angling Methods*, Jenkins, 1935.

West, Leonard. *The Natural Trout Fly and its Imitation*, 1913. Potter, 1921.

Williams, A Courtney. *A Dictionary of Trout Flies*, Black, 1949.

Worlidge, John. *Systema Agriculturae*, 1698.

Young, Andrew. *Anglers Guide to the North of Scotland*, 1857.

Younger, John. *River Angling*, 1840

Acknowledgments

I am deeply grateful to so many people for the advice and information they have given freely in reply to my many questions. In particular to Dr A. M. C. Edwards, Dr G. Mance and Roger Inverarity of the National Rivers Authority; to Leslie Bryan of Trinity College Library, Dublin; Norma Armstrong of the Edinburgh Central Library; C. P. Leftwick of the Fishmongers' Company; Rear Admiral D. J. Mackenzie of the Atlantic Salmon Trust; Ted Hughes; Roy Buckingham; H. G. Edwards of Clifton College; The Law Society of Scotland; Kieran Thompson; John Buckland; Paul S. Panchaud; Sandy Leventon of Salmon and Trout Magazine; Dr Hal Thirlaway of the Piscatorial Society; Fred Buller; T. C. Kingsmill Moore; Mick Lunn of the Houghton Club; Peter Kennedy and Andrew Fisher of the Buccleugh Estates; Paul Windle-Taylor; Kenneth Robson and John Morgan, successively librarians of the Flyfishers' Club library; the Secretary of the Club, Norman Fuller and the President and Committee; Ron Taylor of Fishermen's Feathers; Dr Stephen G. J. Quirke of the British Museum; the photographs from *American Fly Fishing* by Paul Schullery reproduced by permission of Lyons and Burford, publishers, New York; and to Merlin Unwin and my wife for their invaluable help and advice.

183

Index

Aberdeen 39
Aelian 2, 3
Aelfric, Abbot 4
Aestraeus, river 4
Aire, river 110, 111
alder 51, 52
Amber Nymph 174
America 51, 86
colonies 41
American Fly Fishing - see
Schullery
Anglo-Saxon 6
angul 6
Angus 38
angling codes 11
Annan 38
Antrobus Press 19
Apple Tree Fly 50
artificial, minnows 16
Art of Angling, Barker's 41
Ash Fly 50
Ashley-Cooper, John 131
Atlantic Salmon Trust 133, 13

autopsies 61, 62, 114
Awe, river 56

Baillie, James 53-57
Baily's magazine 86
bait 25, 33
bait fishers 31, 48
Ballyshannon 66, 67
Barker 22, 34, 35
*Barker's Delight, or The Art of
Angling* 28, 34, 65
Barker, Thomas 15, 31, 35, 36
Barnes, Dame Juliana - *see*
Berners
Barton, Abbots 88
Bastard Caddis 51
Bates, J. D. 34, 45, 66
bead eyes 45
bear's hair 37, 38, 39
Bell, Dr H. A. 119-121, 125
Bell's Bugs 120, 123
Berners, Dame Juliana 5-7,

11-15, 22, 31, 35, 145
  Berners-type rod 6, 8
  inadequate instructions on fly
  dressings 12
  behaviour of fishermen11,148
Billingsgate Market 36
black country, the 109
Black Gnat 1, 154, 163
Black Leaper 150, 151
Blacker, William 67
Blagdon 119, 120, 124
Blagdon Buzzer 173
Blake, William 109
blowline fishing 105
Blue Charm 70, 72
Blue Dun 33, 42, 51, 63,
  156,159, 168
Blythe, river 59, 60
Borders,the 38, 47, 54, 57, 105
Bossington Mill 91, 113
Bourne, river 105
Bowlker, Richard and Charles 41,
  42, 44, 45, 50, 52, 65
Broughton's Point 53
Bruce, Robert the 65
Bryan, Leslie 66
Bunyan 17
butterflies 45, 46, 73
  Golden Butterfly 67, 70
  Golden Parson 67
Buzzer (midge pupa) 121, 173

Caddis Fly 44
Caddis Pupa 24
Caine, William 77
Calder 111
cane rods 22, 27, 37, 127
Cannon Fly 33, 50
Casting 8, 94
  upstream 9
  false 58
  reach cast 97
Caxton's press 5
Certaine Experiments Concern-
  ing Fish and Fruite 27
chalkstreams 47, 78, 113
  of Hampshire 105
  fishermen 107
Chancery Lane 33
chamois leather 24
Charles II 30
Chepstow 49
Chester Castle 20
Chetham, James 33, 41
Cinnamon Fly 157
Civil War 17, 19
Clifton College 88
Clyde 38
Coln, river 83
Compleat Angler, The 19, 28-30,
  34
conservation 11, 55, 134, 144,
  145

cork 37
Cotton, Charles 19, 26-33, 37, 41, 42
Cox, Mrs, of Winchester 88
Cox, Willie 120
Cray, river 6
Cromwell, Oliver 17, 19, 20, 38
Cutcliffe, H. C. 102

damsel flies, *see* dragon flies
dapping 4, 24
Dark Brown 50
Dark Claret 50
Dark Snipe 162
Dark Watchet 162
dark olive, large 42
Davy, Humphrey 80
Dee, Aberdeenshire 39, 134
Dennys 22
Derbyshire 47, 152
Devon streams 102
dibbling 57
dry fly 9, 10, 22, 23, 50, 51, 58, 81, 83, 86, 88, 89, 99, 100, 105, 106
    technique 84
    avoiding drag 97
    Halford's description 99
    Halford's mistake 99
Dry Fly Fishing in Theory and Practice 93

Dorset 90
Downhill Fly 50
downstream dry fly 96
Dove, river 28, 31, 47, 57, 60, 83, 152, 167
Dovedale 19
dragonflies 35, 44, 45, 73
Drogheda, the seige of 19
Dunblain, Dirty 38
Dun cut 150
Dun fly 149, 151
dunne fly 12
Dunne, J. W. *see* fly designs
Dunbar, Scottish poet 14
Dunkeld 72

Eaton, Mr 62
Edinburgh 39
Edward II 16
emerger 8, 10, 22, 58
entomology 14, 28
Erne 66
eyed hook 88
Experienced Angler, The 19

February Red 13
Field, The 88, 119, 121, 134
fish ponds 28
fish breeding 28
Fishing Gazette 71, 121
fishing rights 14

Fishmonger's Company 14
fixed horsehair line 8, 9
*Floating Flies and How to
   Dress Them* 91
fly designs: 31, 47, 52, 58, 59,
   84, 88, 138
   Cellulite 137
   close imitation 138
   Deane, Peter 139
   Dunne, J. W. 137
   Harding, Colonel E. W. 137
   Halford, F. M. 138
   Modern Dry Fly Code, A 138
   Mottram J. C. 137
   Ronalds, Alfred 138, 155-9
   Schwiebert, Ernest 138
   Skues 137
   Springer, Jenny 137
   Sunshine and the Dry Fly 138
   parachute dressing 138
   precise imitation 138
   Wulff, Lee 139
   Palethorpe, J. A. 139
   Kennet 76, 139
   Swisher and Richards 139
   no-hackle flies 139
   Goddard and Clarke 139
   upside-down flies 139
   Greenwells, Pheasant Tails,
Blue Duns 139
Fly-Fisher's Entomology, The
   59

fly patterns 30
fly fishing tackle:
   space age material 127
   plastic flylines 127
   lead-cored shooting heads 128
   graphite 128
   fiberglass and boron 128
fly fishing philosophy 73, 77,
   78, 80
Foster, David, of Ashbourne 83,
   88
Scientific Angler,The 83
Franck, Colonel Richard 37, 38,
   40, 41, 65
France 41
Francis, Francis 54, 88
   The Field 54
French Revolution 54
*Fysshynge Wyth an Angle
   Treatyse of* 5-7, 12-15, 52

gaff 35, 38
Garry Dog 71
Gay, John 47, 48
Germany 106
George II 41
George Inn:
   at Aldersgate 21, 28, 88
Gingrich, Arnold 5
Glasgow 38
Gold-Ribbed Hare's Ear 97, 99

Golden Dun Midge 158
Gordon, Theodore 51, 101
Graeco-Roman hooks 4, 44
   plumes 16
Green Drake 31, 33, 168
Green Midge 174
Greene, Plunket, Harry 106, 107
Greenwell's Glory 120, 139
Grey Drake 31, 33
Grenadier, the 121
Grey, Sir Edward 78, 80, 90
   Viscount, of Fallodon 77, 79
Grouse Hackle 53
Grouse and Yellow 55
Guildhall 14, 36

Hairy Mary 72
Hall, H. S. 50, 86-88
   split-wing floaters 85
Halford, F. M. 23, 51, 83, 87,
   90, 91, 93, 94, 96, 105, 113
   dry fly code 101
   death of 102
Hammonds' tackle shop 86
   88, 90
Hampshire rivers 44
Hardy cayalogue 133
hatch of a fly 27
Hawthorn fly 154
Heddon, Jack 5, 49
Highlands, the 39

Hispaniola 20
History of Fishing for Trout, A -
   see Waller Hills
Hofland's Fancy 53
Holburn 6
Holland of Salisbury 88
Honeydun Press 49
horsehair line 7-9, 24, 26, 55,
   57, 58
   tapered 22, 51, 59
Houghton Club 91
Hills, *see* Waller Hills

Illingworth, A. H. 123
imago 53
imitation, exact 25, 61, 93
   bait 120, 121
Ireland 19, 39, 44, 47, 65
iron blue 50, 63, 99, 107

Jacques, David 100
Jamaica 20
Jed, river 101
Joad, Professor 83
Jock Scott 70, 165
Johnson, Dr 41
Jones, Inigo 34
Kelson, George 44, 70-75
   salmon flies 131, 163-6
Kennedy, Peter 65

King's Fisher 45
Kingsmill Moore, T. C. 78, 80

La Branche, George 102-104
Lascelles 50
Lawrie 13, 19, 26
Lawson, William 37
Leeds 110, 111
Leonard, Hiram 86
Leven, Earl of 38
Leven, loch 56, 112
libella, *see* dragon flies
Linnaeus, Carl 42
London 6, 14, 20, 36, 44
   rivers 14
Ludlow 41
Lyons, Nick 80

Macedon 2
   Macedonians 3, 12
mayfly 14
McCaskie, H. B. 75, 101
McClane, A. L. 128
Mckay 44, 66, 67, 70
magic potions 31, 40
Malham Tarn 110
Malone, E. J. 65
mallard flies 120
Manchester 112
March Brown 13, 106

Markham 22
Marinaro, Vincent 138
Marryat, G. S. 50, 87, 88, 90,
   91, 96
Marlborough 78
Marston, R. B. 71
Marshall, Howard 81
Master of Game, The 5
Mascall 22
Maure Fly 150, 151
McDonald, John 12
minnow, artificial 16
Montague, Lord 34
Moore, *see* Kingsmill Moore
Morawski, Mrs Winnie 131
moth 45, 46
Muir:
   William, of Innistrynich 56

naming of flies 50
Napoleonic Wars 54
National Rivers Authority 112,
   143
natural fly 27, 28
Nelson, Lord 113
Newsom, Eric 120
New York 104
Nickson, Sir David 134
Nith, river 38
Northern Memoirs 38
Norris, Thaddeus 102

nymph 35, 42, 53, 99, 116
  fishing 24, 26, 100

O'Gorman 44
Ogden, James, of Cheltenham 83
Orange Partridge 53
Orange Quill 23
Overfield, D. 93

Parker, C. G. A. 19
peacock's feathers 39
Peacock Fly 45, 50
Pennsylvania 104
Piscatorial Society 129
Preshute bridge 78
Princess of Wales 72
point and two droppers 50
pollution:
  of rivers 109, 141
  acid rain 141, 142
  Department of the
    Environment 142
  farm chemicals and silage 142
  George, Dr Martin 142
  Independent, The 143
  Nature Conservancy 142
  Norfolk Broads 142
  Royal Commission on
    Environmental Pollution,

1987   111, 142
  Royal Society study 141
  Tamar, on 141
  Test 143
  Times, The 142
  plumes 1, 2, 16, 35, 72
  Public Health in Leeds - see
    Toft
  public water supply reservoirs
    112
  Pulman, George 83, 89, 90

Rawson, Stephen 106
Radcliffe 3, 16
Red Fly 50
Restoration poets 30
reservoir fishing 119, 123
  Behrendt, Alex 124
  Bristol Waterworks 124
  Crawford, Colonel J. K. B.
    124
  Dr Bell 119-121
  effects of threadlining 123
  fly-only rules 124
  Ivens, T. C. 125
  Two Lakes 124
rivercraft 23, 27, 34, 42, 55,
  57-61, 94, 103
River Pollution, Louis Klein 112
roach fishers 14
Rogan 44, 67

Romans, the 2, 15, 35
  plumes 13
Ronalds, Alfred 51, 52, 59, 63,
  155-9
Royal Society, the 42, 80
running line of shoemaker's
  thread 26
running lines and reels 27, 35,
  36, 38
Rural Sports see Gay

Salter 49
salmon 14-16, 24, 33, 34, 38,
  39, 42, 45
  fishing 16, 34, 132
  flies 24, 34, 35, 39, 44-46, 66
  The Salmon Fly 68
  rods and tackle 22, 34, 46
  fishing rights 65
  Women's wear for 72
Salmon Fisher's Odyssey
  see - Ashley-Cooper
Salmon and Trout Association
  135
Salisbury, the George Inn 21
Sawyer, Frank 115, 116, 119
  Pheasant Tail Nymph 116
seatrout 51
Schwiebert, Ernest *see* fly
  designs
Scientific Angler, The

  - see Foster
Scott, Jock 70, 165
Scotland 38, 47, 65, 101
  salmon fishing 39, 65
  rivers of 39
  flydressers in 131
Scotcher, George 49, 52, 57, 59,
  106
Schullery, Paul 84, 128
sedge 14
Seine estuary 16
Severn, river 41, 46
sewin - *see* seatrout
Shakespeare, William 17
Shannon, river 66
Sheffield 112
Sheringham, H. T. 75, 119
silk line 55, 57, 86
silkworm gut 57
six-sided split cane rod 86
Shipley, William 57, 166
Shropshire 44
Simpson, John 49
snelled hooks 88
Smith, General Bedell 66
Spey 68
spiders 54
  Black 55
  Dun 55
  Red 55
spliced rod 55
split-wing floater 88, 105

starling wings 33
Stewart, W. C. 47, 53-56, 62, 93, 94, 102, 105
streamer flies, *see* plumes
St Bertin, Abbey of 4
stiff hackle 88
Stirling 39
Stoddart, Tom 68
Stone Fly 14, 31
Skues, G. E. M. 13, 23, 61, 86, 88, 89, 105, 114-116, 119, 120
  dry fly 113
  Minor Tactics of the Chalk Stream 113
  Blue Dun 114
  wet fly 114
  upstream 113, 114
  nymphs 114, 115
  marrow spoon 114, 120
  emerger patterns 116
spinner 23, 53
split-wing floaters 88, 172-3
sub-imago 42
Sussex 120

Tay, river 134
Taverner, John 22, 27, 28, 35, 37
teal wing 38
Teal and Green 55
Tees, river 111
Teme, river 41, 44

Test, river 91, 106
Teviot, rivers 53
Thames, river 6, 14, 16, 33, 36, 46
Thorn Tree Fly 152
Thornton, Col 76
Three Trouts, St Paul's Churchyard 20, 33, 36
timeshare 133
Toft, Wohl 110
Traherne 69
Treatyse - see *Fysshynge Wyth An Angle*
Trevelyan, G. M. 17, 41, 75
triple gut 55
trout flies 36
trolling 26, 56
Toby spoons 16
tube fly 131, 132
Tweed, river 39, 68, 101, 141
Tyburn, river 6
Tyne, river 16

Usk, river 68
upside-down flies 23
upstream wet fly 53, 55, 57, 113, 119, 161
  on fast rivers 102
ultra purists 94
Uttoxeter 59

Variegated Sun Fly 71, 164
Venables, Robert 18-23, 26, 27,
    37, 47, 49, 66, 106, 151

Waddington, Richard 132
Wales, south 57
Waller Hills, J. *History of
    Fishing for Trout* 6, 7, 13, 27,
    38, 47, 91, 93,109
Walton, Izaak 9, 17, 20-1,
    28-31, 34, 36, 41, 48, 152
    Compleat Angler 15, 17, 41,
    152, 153
    ironmonger's shop 33
Wanless, Arthur 123
Wasp Fly 150-51
water-bred flies 42
water knot 55
water meadows 76
waterproof:
    fishing boots 60, 73
    stockings 55
Wandle, river 6, 14
weed cutting 105
wet fly 9, 22, 52, 58, 59, 93,
100, 161
    counter-revolution of 105
    downstream 60
    upstream 161
Westbourne brook 6
Westminster 14, 34, 110

Abbey archives 5
weighted caddis pupa 25
wharf 101
Whitehall 34, 36
White Horse hill 78
white water 101
whipping the line 9
Wigan, Michael 134
Wildbad, river 106
Willet, Mark 49, 154
Wilson, Dermot 96, 169
Winchester, *see* George Inn at
    Aldersgate
winch 26
winder 34
Woodcock Fly 50
Woodcock and Orange 55
Worlidge, John 57
Wright, James 33
Wright of Sprouston-on-Tweed
    131
Wynkyn de Worde 6, 13
Wye, river 46

Yale University library 5
Yorkshire, West 110
Younger, John 116, 118
    *River Angling for Salmon and
    Trout* 116

Zulus 106

The following books are also published by:
Merlin Unwin Books, 21 Corve Street, Ludlow
Shropshire SY8 1DA

A Passion for Angling
Chris Yates, Bob James, Hugh Miles

This beautifully illustrated book, accompanied by the major BBC TV series of the same name, tells the story of an angling adventure which takes three fishing pals across Britain in quest of salmon, trout, barbel, carp, tench, roach, pike and pretty well every freshwater species. The story of their exploits - entertainingly told by Chris Yates - is not to be missed.

Complementing the fabulous colour photos, there are 39 specially-commissioned wash illustrations by the artist Rodger McPhail.

£16.99 ISBN 0563367415

Oliver Edwards' Flytyers Masterclass
a step-by-step guide to tying 20 essential patterns for the flyfisher
Oliver Edwards

This book, the result of 30 years of field research into insect-life and a similar length of time experimenting with techniques and materials at the vice, tells you how to tie 20 key flies using all the most up-to-date techniques. By following the author's clear sequential drawings, you will be able to create your own superb artificial flies. Techniques explained include: making dubbing loops, nylon-backed caddis wings, 'Mohican' winging, permanently-splayed nymph tails, patterns from foam, etc.

£19.99 ISBN 1 873674 08 2

Bernard Venables
the illustrated memoirs of a fisherman
Bernard Venables

Bernard Venables is a remarkable angler by the standards of any generation. In his time he has caught record fish, he was a co-founder and director of *Angling Times*, probably the most successful fishing journal of modern times, he founded the popular but short-lived magazine *Creel*, he invented the cartoon character Mr Crabtree (the inspiration of so many budding anglers), he regularly broadcast on television (*Angler's Corner*) and radio and, last but by no means least, he is a distinguished artist whose paintings (many of which have been of fish, rivers, anglers and lakes) are much sought after by collectors.

He has known and fished with the likes of Richard Walker, Charles Ritz, Frank Sawyer, Oliver Kite, Terry Thomas, Lionel Sweet - indeed many of the most famous fishing personalities of the past 60 years. His clear recollection of conversations and adventures in their company are wonderful to read.

This beautifully illustrated book - part angler's autobiography, part artist's retrospective - will delight all Venables fans. It is the testimony, in pictures and words, of one of the great angling characters of the twentieth century.

Price: £19.95   ISBN: 1 873674 06 6

The Secret Carp
Chris Yates

'Unquestionably the read of the year, indeed of many years. It is a potential classic.' - The Times.

Now available in paperback, the acclaimed story of Chris Yates's thrilling and wonderfully atmospheric day and night at a carp lake. A book for *all* anglers to enjoy.

Price: £9.95 ISBN 1 873674 11 2

Trout and Salmon Rivers of Ireland

an angler's guide

Peter O'Reilly

This deeply-researched guide to the rivers of Ireland has been eagerly awaited by game anglers. Since the phenomenal success of his first book, *Trout and Salmon Loughs of Ireland* (a No.1 bestseller in Ireland), Peter O'Reilly has been painstakingly gathering information on the rivers.

Most of the material contained in this book has never before been published so its concise presentation in book form provides the angler with an exciting opportunity to discover some of Europe's best kept fishing secrets.

The rivers are described in great detail - their geographical characteristics, the most productive stretches, game species present, stock levels and average size, catch records when known, local permit requirements (names and addresses given whenever possible), best flies to use, open and close season dates, best fishing times in the year - and much more.

Ordnance Survey references accompany each river entry and detailed location maps (many showing bridges, beats, access roads, etc.) are provided for every significant river in the Republic and Northern Ireland, enabling the angler to plan fishing expeditions in meticulous detail.

No angler of Ireland's rivers should be without this superb new guide.

Peter O'Reilly is Angling Officer at the Central Fisheries Board and is widely recognised as a leading authority on Ireland's trout, sea-trout and salmon fishing. He writes for various angling publications, including regular features and reports in *Trout and Salmon*, *Salmon Trout & Seatrout* and the *Atlantic Salmon Journal*.

Price: £16.95   ISBN:1 873674 01 5

The Pursuit of Wild Trout

Mike Weaver

Fishing for wild trout in unspoilt waters is for Mike Weaver - and a growing number of anglers - the ultimate fishing experience. The fish may not be as large as those from the nearby stocked fishery but what they lack in weight they make up for in fighting quality and sharp-finned, speckled beauty. For the game angler, the author argues, small really is beautiful and a day spent wild trouting is both challenging and rewarding.

This beautifully illustrated book from one of Britain's leading writers on wild trout fishing is for the angler who places quality before mere size, who regards beautiful scenery as a vital ingredient in the fishing day and who is happy to practice 'catch-and-release' in the interest of maintaining stocks of wild fish.

Mike Weaver is a thoughtful and experimental angler and his tactics for out-witting 'wildies' - whether brown, rainbow, brook or cutthroat - are always practical and clearly presented.

From the Tamar, Lyn and Teign in the West Country, to the rainbow-breeding Derbyshire Wye, to the limestone Suir in Ireland and some exciting trout rivers in the USA - the geographical range of this book is wide - Mike Weaver always draws on his first-hand experience.

He discusses the use of barbless hooks, deep wading, innovative fly-tying techniques to 'match the hatch', the classic standard patterns and a variety of stream fishing methods that really do catch trout.

Price: £16.95 ISBN:1873674007

The One That Got Away

or tales of days when fish triumphed over anglers

With original woodcuts by Christopher Wormell

'The one that got away' is the best-known phrase in fishing. Every angler has at least one story of being outwitted by a huge fish. A refrain of the angler, a taunt from those who live with them; it neatly sums up the way in which anglers are obsessed with the fish they almost caught. Yet to hear a fisherman tell the story of an escapee leviathon is to gain a great insight into why he fishes in the first place and why his sport is the most popular in the world.

This is a collection of original stories from well-known angling enthusiasts and writers. They tell of unforgettable fish hooked and lost, of glimpsed monsters which haunt the imagination and draw the narrator back to a particular lake or river, time and again, in search of a re-match.

David Steel loses his first-ever salmon after an epic struggle on the Ettrick, George Melly is upstaged by a giant Usk brown trout, Jeremy Paxman describes a hilarious adventure in Sri Lanka, Max Hastings battles it out on the Naver, Bernard Venables - extending the definition of 'fish' - describes a thrilling but tragic whaling adventure in the Azores. Chris Yates, holder of the British carp record, tells of his close encounter with an even bigger carp, David Profumo is humiliated by a 400lb shark, Brian Clarke has his angling life marked by a monster pike and Conrad Voss Bark actually helped his fish get away - and he swears it came back to say 'thank you'.

The pens of sixteen of the finest fishing writers have been at work and the result makes compelling reading for anglers of every persuasion.

Price: £16.95 ISBN: 1-873674-02-3

An Angler for all Seasons

the best of H. T. Sheringham

H. T. Sheringham ranks among the finest fishing writers of the twentieth century. Here is a collection of the very best of his angling experiences, taken mainly from his six fishing books and from *The Field*, for which he was angling editor.

No fish escaped his interest, even if it did sometimes escape his creel - carp, tench, chub, pike, roach, salmon and trout - all were pursued with equal gusto.

He takes the reader on a journey without frontiers, from the reservoirs (Blagdon in its opening years) to the finest chalkstreams in England, from overgrown canals to Welsh salmon rivers. No snob, he knew only the joy of the sport.

He is funny, he is moving and - most rare - he is modest about his all-round skills with rod and line. If you are new to Sheringham, *An Angler for all Seasons* will convert you into one of his many admirers.

In 1903, while fishing on the Lambourn, Sheringham met William Senior, the Editor of *The Field*, and was offered the job of Angling Editor of that magazine. It was a job he held until his death in 1930, at the age of 54.

Besides his regular magazine articles, he wrote several novels and six fishing books, including *An Angler's Hours*, *An Open Creel*, *Elements of Angling*, *Coarse Fishing*, *Trout Fishing: Memories and Morals* and *Fishing: its Cause, Treatment and Cure*.

He wrote with passion about the pleasures of coarse fishing which, unusually for his generation, he rated as highly as trout and salmon fishing.

The essays in this anthology have been chosen and introduced by Tom Fort, the angling correspondent of the *Financial Times*.

Price £16.95   ISBN: 1 873674 04 X